Crafting Your Dream Career

The 7 Success Mantras to Transform Your Life into a Rewarding Traditional Science Career

Dr. Swarnangini Sinha

Copyright © 2024 Swarnangini Sinha

All rights reserved. No part of this book may be used or reproduced in any form whatsoever without written permission except in the case of brief quotations in critical articles or reviews.

For more information contact at:

Email ID: swarnangini@gmail.com

Linkedin ID: https://www.linkedin.com/in/dr-swarnangini-sinha/

Facebook ID: https://www.facebook.com/swarna.sinha.33

ISBN:9798301401909

DEDICATION

I dedicate this book to my late parents, who devoted their lives to improving society. I am genuinely grateful for their influence in shaping me into a person who can contribute

CONTENTS

	Acknowledgments	I
1	Introduction	1
2	Your Roadmap: Book Series Framework	10
3	Breaking Career Myths	15
4	Raising Your Belief: You can do it!	21
5	From Goals to Growth	30
6	The Challenging Landscape of Career	36
7	The Success Mantras	42
8	Discover Your Career Path	50
9	Exploring Exciting Career Paths	57
10	Connecting and Mentoring	63
11	The Power of Learning and Technology	68
12	Research Tools and Global Collaborations	72
13	Skill Development for Life	77

14	The Digital Edge and Technology Wonders	82
15	Medical and Health Sciences	86
16	Engineering and Technology	108
17	Pure Sciences	131
18	Research and Development	155
	Essential Resources	179
	• Websites for Career Research	181
	• Books for Career Research	183
	• Professional Networks	185
	• Scholarships in India and Abroad	188
	• Trainings in India and Abroad	195
	• Research Grants and Fellowships	200
	• Online Learning Platforms	205
	• Professional Associations and Societies	211
	• Government Initiatives and Programs	216
	• Exploring Top Universities for Your Dream Career	220

ACKNOWLEDGMENTS

I want to thank Pakhi, my daughter, my constant supporter and honest critic, whose faith in me inspired this book. Her encouragement and belief that young minds need guidance at this crucial life stage gave me the courage to share my journey and help students shape their dreams.

A special thank you to my husband for his support. I am also thankful to Ms. Sweta Samota, Founder and Coach, India Authors Academy for her incredible mentorship.

Lastly, my deepest appreciation goes to the readers. Your feedback will help shape future editions of this work.

INTRODUCTION

"Your work is going to fill a large part of your life, and the only way to be truly satisfied is to do what you believe is great work. And the only way to do great work is to love what you do."

- Steve Jobs

1 INTRODUCTION

"Your career is not defined by what you find, but by what you create through passion and purpose".

-Simon Sinek

Congratulations on completing 10+2!

It's a significant achievement, and feeling uncertain as you plan your next steps is normal. Crafting Your Dream Career is here to guide you through this exciting time. Career planning is essential because it aligns your unique skills and passions with the opportunities that will bring you joy and success.

Let us take inspiration from young leaders who have made their dreams a reality. Consider **Tilak Mehta**, a young entrepreneur from India. At 13, Tilak founded **Papers N Parcels**, a Mumbai-based courier service that uses the **Dabbawala Network**. His idea was simple but powerful: offer quick, same-day delivery within the city. Today, his company helps thousands by delivering important documents and packages within hours.

What makes Tilak's journey inspiring is his ability to see a problem and come up with a creative solution despite his young age. He didn't wait until he was older or had more experience-he saw an opportunity and acted. It teaches us an important lesson: success is not always about age or years of experience but about finding opportunities and having the courage to pursue them.

Similarly, **Shradha Khapra**, known as **'Microsoft Wali Didi**,' took a bold step when she left a high-paying job at Microsoft to co-found Apna College, a YouTube channel dedicated to helping students navigate their academic journeys. Her decision wasn't easy; she faced questions from family and friends who questioned her choice to leave stability for uncertainty. Yet, driven by her passion for education, Shraddha has made a significant impact, empowering countless students.

These individuals remind us that crafting a career that brings success and personal satisfaction is possible with the right mindset and dedication. Their stories aren't just about fame or wealth; they highlight pursuing your passion and staying committed.

Statistics and Career Mismatches:
As we celebrate these success stories, we must acknowledge the challenges many students face regarding career choices. A 2020 survey found that 93% of students knew only a few common career paths, often leading to mismatches. For instance, 50% of engineering graduates in India work outside their field of study. Globally, nearly 45% of workers are in jobs

that don't match their skill sets.

This disconnect between career goals and reality can have serious consequences. In India, 33% of graduates couldn't find jobs in 2022 because their skills didn't match market demands. That's why discovering a career that aligns with your interests is essential, creating a future where your passions and abilities can excel.

My Journey:
Reflecting on these challenges, I can relate deeply to finding one's path. I come from a middle-class family, where both my parents had humble beginnings. My mother, in particular, faced significant financial hardships growing up in a family of 12 siblings. Yet, she became the first person in her locality to graduate, overcoming challenges that would have discouraged many.

Her devotion to uplifting others inspired me as I witnessed her determination to make a difference. After working as a Central government employee during the day, she dedicated her evenings to teaching women and children in the village, leading to the birth of the Uday Night School. Her dedication deeply influenced my values and instilled in me the importance of education and community service.

In my 25+ years of teaching, I have visited many schools, particularly in Madhya Pradesh, where I've observed students struggling with limited career options. It's disheartening to see that even in countries as advanced as the U.S., many parents make career decisions for their children, leaving them uncertain about their ambitions.

It inspired me to write this book series to connect with students globally and help them discover their dream careers.

I also wanted to set an example for my daughter, showing her that if you consistently follow your passion and love what you do, you can shape your desired career.

Real-Life Success Stories:
To further illustrate this journey, let's look at more young people who have successfully navigated their challenges and achieved their dreams. For example, **Zaynab Younes** from Lebanon initially pursued a civil engineering career. However, during her studies, she realized her true passion lay in sustainable energy solutions. After completing her degree, she started working on solar energy projects in rural areas, helping communities gain access to renewable energy. Her innovative approach and commitment to sustainability led her to receive global recognition, making her a role model for young people aspiring to make a difference in the world through technology and environmental progress.

Likewise, **Amara Okoye** from Nigeria experienced her transformation. Attending a climate change workshop shifted her focus from studying law to renewable energy. Despite initial resistance from her family, she launched a startup providing affordable solar power to rural communities. Her journey highlights the courage it takes to follow one's heart, and her impact on improving lives reflects that bravery.

These stories remind us that the path to success is not always straightforward. Finding your passion and pursuing it with focus can lead to unexpected satisfaction. Each journey is unique, yet the common thread is dedication and a desire to create a career that aligns with personal values.

Quick Reflection!
Take a moment to reflect on your passions.
- What excites you?
- What drives your curiosity?
- Write down your top three passions and consider how they could guide you toward potential career options.

This exploration is an essential step in your journey.

The Dark Side of Wrong Career Choices:
Considering the importance of aligning passions with career paths, we must recognize the darker side of mismatched choices. In Kota, Rajasthan, the intense pressure surrounding exam performance has tragically led to an increase in student suicides. This challenging reality highlights the importance of early career guidance and the need for a supportive environment for students as they navigate their futures.

However, even under such pressure, inspiring success stories emerge. **Carlos Ramirez** from Mexico chose filmmaking despite societal expectations to pursue engineering. Despite financial struggles and doubt from peers, he persisted, and today, his films are celebrated at international festivals, inspiring others to chase their dreams.

Similarly, **Rajeev Kumar** once pursued medicine and found his true calling in social work. His shift from the medical field to educational reform has significantly improved access to education for underprivileged children in his community, demonstrating the life-changing power of following one's passion.

These examples remind us that pursuing what you love can lead to remarkable outcomes despite challenges.

A Heartfelt Message to You

Dear Champ,

Life's difficulties may sometimes feel challenging, especially when you are trying to understand your future. Your parents care deeply about you, and sometimes that brings stress. Talk to someone you trust if you are unsure or stressed. Remember, difficulties are a part of life, but so is hope. Stay true to what you love, and remember you are building an extraordinary future.

A Message to Parents

As a professor, I have always valued discipline, excellence, and perfection. Naturally, I expected the same from my daughter, who excelled in public speaking, dance, music, and karate. But in pushing her to be perfect, I unknowingly put too much pressure on her. Over time, this created a distance between us. She started hiding things from me, and her performance in school began to suffer. Eventually, her teachers told me she was leaving her exam papers blank. Because she could not handle the extreme exam pressure, and she used to forget everything due to blackouts.

It was a wake-up call. I realized I had been focusing too much on my daughter's achievements and not enough on her well-being. We sought medical help for her anxiety and self-esteem issues, and that's when I truly began to understand how important mental health is.

Growing up, I didn't know much about "anxiety" or "depression". I used to think these were just excuses for not working hard. But my daughter's experience changed that for me. Mental health is natural, and it affects many children, especially when they feel overwhelmed by the pressure we, parents or teachers, might unintentionally put on them.

I'm sharing this not just as an educator but as a mother who learned a valuable lesson. My advice to all parents and teachers is simple: please be kind to your children. Encourage them, understand their dreams, and give them the love and trust they need. Let's be their role models and ensure they feel supported, safe, and proud of themselves.

Watching your child grow and make important decisions is both rewarding and challenging. While It's normal to want the best for them, it's essential to support their dreams. It will help them create a future that reflects their true selves, not just what society expects.

As you and your child explore the future, remember there are so many opportunities. It's not just about finding a job-It's about building a happy and satisfying life. This book will guide you through the process, helping you discover and open doors to endless possibilities.

Now is the time to start imagining, exploring, and taking the first steps toward a meaningful and passionate future. The power to build your dream career is in your hands, and the best time to begin is now.

Final Thoughts:
- Follow what excites you, and success will follow.
- Be bold, take risks, and trust in your abilities.
- Align your passions with your career to avoid mismatches.
- Open conversations with support from loved ones make all the difference.
- Starting each step brings you closer to your dream career.

YOUR ROADMAP: BOOK SERIES FRAMEWORK

"The best way to predict the future is to create it."

- Peter Drucker

2 YOUR ROADMAP: BOOK SERIES FRAMEWORK

"**A framework turns vision into action and dreams into reality.**"

- Tony Robbins

As you step into life after 10+2, the book series "**Planning Your Dream Career**" will guide you through the exciting options in science careers. We have 12 books covering seven essential areas: Traditional Science Careers, the Latest Technology, New Healthcare Careers, Interdisciplinary Science Careers, Sustainable Development and Environmental Careers, Innovative Technology Careers, Innovative Science Entrepreneurship, and Unconventional and Futuristic Careers. From exploring marine biology to the future of AI, we'll help you find where your interests can lead you. Whether you're excited about working with the newest technology or making a difference in sustainable development, this series will help you every step of the way. Let's start exploring your future together!

How this Book Series can help you?

A Full Exploration of Career Paths:
The world of science careers goes far beyond traditional jobs. New fields are growing daily with technology and a more significant focus on sustainability. This book series explores over 1,000 career options, including AI, data science, environmental sustainability, and biotechnology. You'll learn about:

- Qualifications: What education and training is essential for different careers?
- Academic Programs: The best programs and institutions for special training.
- Growth Opportunities: Future outlook and career growth possibilities.
- Job Options: Where and how you can use your skills.
- Top Companies: Leading companies in each field.
- Salaries: Expected pay and income growth.
- Renowned Universities: Famous universities that offer specific programs.
- Important Skills: Key skills you need to succeed in your chosen career.

Solving Your Career Confusion:
Choosing a career can be challenging, and many students need help. This book will help you with:
Lack of Knowledge: Learn about different careers you may not have heard of.

- Mismatch in Education and Career: See how your studies can lead to the right career.
- Career Happiness: Find a career that fits what you enjoy and are good at.

Choosing the right career can be stressful, but always remember: **Your happiness matters most.**

Real-Life Success Stories:
Includes inspiring stories from people who have faced career struggles, offering:
- Inspiration: How others have turned their interests into successful careers.
- Useful Tips: Learn from their experiences and use their methods.

Helping Parents and Teachers:
A helpful tool for understanding and supporting students in their career choices.
- Help for Parents: How to support your child in making intelligent decisions about their future.
- Tools for Teachers: Knowledge to guide students in the right way.

Simple and Friendly Content:
Books are written in a friendly and easy-to-understand style, making complex information simple.
Whether you're a student, parent, or teacher, you'll find the content engaging and easy to follow.

A Great Choice for Your Future:
By getting this book, you're not just buying a guide but making a smart choice for your future. The information you learn will help you:
- Provide Clarity: Help you make informed choices about your career.
- Save Time: Avoid mistakes by following a well-researched guide.
- Boost Confidence: Give you the knowledge needed to follow your dreams.

Imagine waking up every day excited about your work. Thoughtful career planning makes this possible by connecting your work with your passions and strengths.

The first book in this series, **Crafting Your Dream Career,** serves as your trusted guide on your career journey, providing valuable knowledge and practical advice. Whether you're just starting to think about your future or looking to make a change, this book is here to support you every step of the way.

So, are you ready to take the first step toward shaping the career of your dreams? Let's begin the journey and start building the future you deserve today!

Final Thoughts:
- Explore various career options and find the one that excites you.
- Don't let confusion hold you back from discovering careers that align with your passions.
- Real-life success stories show that your dreams are possible with the right mindset.
- Parents and teachers, you guide students toward smart career choices.

Start today; this series will give you the clarity and confidence to build a career you love.

BREAKING CAREER MYTHS

"It's not what you achieve, it's what you overcome. That's what defines your career."

- Carlton Fisk

3 BREAKING CAREER MYTHS

"Have the courage to follow your heart and intuition."

- Steve Jobs

In the first chapter, we discussed how important it is to plan your career and how matching your interests with your career choices can lead to a happy life. We also discussed the effect of careful career planning and shared real-life stories that show the power of choosing a career you love.

Let us look at some common false ideas that might stop you from making intelligent and confident career decisions.

What if everything you knew about careers was wrong?
Many of us grow up hearing specific ideas about careers that shape how we think. But what if these ideas are only partly true? Let's challenge some of the most common myths holding you back.

Myth 1: You must choose a career path early

Choosing a career path early in your life can be helpful, but It's not something you have to do forever. Many successful people change careers later and find even more happiness in new fields. Being open and ready to learn can lead to great opportunities.

Jeff Bezos, Executive Chairman of Amazon:

Jeff Bezos began his career in finance, working at investment firms before starting Amazon at 30. His move from finance to creating one of the world's biggest e-commerce companies shows that It's never too late to change careers.

Myth 2: High-paying jobs are always the best choice

A good salary is essential, but finding a job that makes you happy matters too. A high-paying job that doesn't match your interests can make you tired and unhappy.

Ratan Tata, Chairman Emeritus of Tata Sons:

Ratan Tata could have stayed in high-paying roles, but he focused on making a more significant impact through his leadership. His choice shows that the value of a career isn't just about the money but also the difference it makes.

Myth 3: Only specific careers are respected

Respect in a job comes from how much it fits your values and how passionate you are about it. Any work that helps society is respected, no matter what others think.

Gordon Ramsay, Michelin Starred Chef and TV Personality:

Gordon Ramsay started as a football player but turned to cooking after an injury. His choice to become a chef, once seen as a less important career, has made him a global icon in cooking.

Myth 4: Failing in a career means you've made the wrong choice

Failing doesn't mean you've chosen the wrong career. It's part of the journey to success. You can achieve even greater success by learning from your failures and changing how you do things.

Thomas Edison, inventor and founder of General Electric:

Thomas Edison failed many times before he finally invented the light bulb. His hard work shows how important it is to learn from failures and keep trying.

Myth 5: You need to have everything figured out from the start

It's completely okay not to have everything planned out from the start. Career paths can be full of surprises, and you'll find what fits you best through exploring and gaining skills.

Masako Wakamiya, App Developer and Technology Enthusiast:

Masako Wakamiya didn't start her career in technology until she was in her 60s. She is now known as one of the world's oldest app developers, proving that age is no barrier to new ideas.

Myth 6: Only degrees from well-known universities lead to success

While top universities can offer great chances, success isn't just about where you graduate from. Your skills, experience, and hard work often matter more than the name of your degree.

Mark Zuckerberg, cofounder of Facebook:
Mark Zuckerberg left Harvard University to focus on building his company. His success shows that skills, vision, and determination can lead to remarkable achievements, regardless of the university name.

By breaking these myths, I hope to help you move past ideas that might stop you and find a career that excites you. Remember, your career journey is your own, shaped by what you love, value, and your choices.

These are just a few myths that can confuse you when choosing your career path. You can take control of your future by understanding and getting past them. Remember, you have the power to create your path, and with careful planning, there's no limit to your impact.

Final Thoughts:
- It's always possible to change your career path and find success.
- A rewarding job matters more than a high salary-happiness leads to success.
- Respect comes from passion and impact, not just from job titles.
- Failure is a stepping stone-learn from it and keep moving forward.
- You don't need to have everything figured out immediately-explore, grow, and adopt surprises.

RAISING YOUR BELIEF: YOU CAN DO IT

"Believe you can and you're halfway there."

- Theodore Roosevelt.

4 RAISING YOUR BELIEF: YOU CAN DO IT

"Challenges are what make life interesting, and overcoming them is what makes life meaningful."

- Joshua J. Marine

In the earlier chapters, we discussed why career planning matters and cleared up some myths that could get in your way. Now, let us explore the real problems you might face while chasing your dream career. Understanding these issues and how to handle them is critical to building the dream career you want.

Why is reaching your dream career so tough?
Many people find the path to a happy career filled with problems. These problems, both inside yourself and from outside, can feel like too much to handle. But by seeing the issues, knowing what's holding you back, and using simple ways to fix them, you can clear these barriers and confidently move toward your goals.

Let us discuss some Common Problems and Fears in achieving your Dream Career.

Fear of Failure:
Many people are afraid of failing if they go after a challenging career. This fear can be so intense that it makes them settle for less than they want.

Winning Formula:
Instead of fearing failure, see it as a step to success. Research shows that those who take risks and learn from their failures are more likely to succeed in the long run.

Think of **Elon Musk.** Before starting SpaceX and Tesla, Musk had many setbacks and failed businesses. His strength and ability to learn from these failures helped him build some of the world's most successful companies.

Success Hack:
Start with small, manageable goals that build up to your bigger career dreams. Celebrate your progress, and when setbacks happen, use them as chances to learn and grow, just like Musk did.

Not Knowing About Career Options:
Many students and young professionals need to be aware of all the different career paths they could take. This lack of knowledge can limit their future and lead to choices they might later regret.

Winning Formula:
Broaden your perspective by exploring different fields and industries. Do your research, attend career fairs, talk to

professionals, and find advisors who can share insights about various career paths.

A great example is **Moziah Bridges**, who started his bow tie business, Mo's Bows, at nine years old. Moziah wanted stylish bow ties but couldn't find any he liked, so he decided to make his own. Even though he was young, his creativity and business-minded spirit helped him build a successful fashion brand. His story shows how knowing about different career opportunities from a young age and following your passions can lead to great success.

Success Hack:
Set aside time each week to learn about different careers. Use online resources, seek career counselling, and talk to people to expand your understanding of what's out there, just like Moziah explored his options.

Parental Pressure:
Sometimes, parents push their kids toward careers that don't match their true interests, leading to frustration and a lack of excitement.

Winning Formula:
Honest talks can make a big difference. Speak openly with your parents about what you're passionate about and the career path you want to follow. Share real-life examples to show them that non-traditional careers can also be successful.

For example, **Malavath Poorna**, an Indian mountaineer, became the youngest girl to climb Mount Everest at 13. Even though her parents wanted her to focus on her studies, Poorna followed her love for mountaineering and convinced them to support her dream. Her success shows how following your passion, even with parental pressure, can lead to incredible achievements.

Success Hack:
Make a list of people who followed different career paths and succeeded. Share this with your parents during your talks to help calm their worries and support your choices, just like Poorna did by showing her commitment.

Imposter Syndrome:
Feeling like a fake, even when you have proof that you're good enough, can cause self-doubt and hesitation about pursuing big goals.

Winning Formula:
Remember, feeling like a fake is something many successful people experience. For example, **Emma Watson** has said that she sometimes feels she doesn't deserve her success, even though she has achieved a lot. Her story shows you can still push through and reach your goals even when you think this way.

Success Hack:
Start a journal to record your wins and the positive things people say about you. When self-doubt arises, look back at your journal to remind yourself of your successes and capability, just like Watson finds ways to believe in her achievements.

Fear of the Unknown:
Starting a new or unfamiliar career can feel challenging. The fear of what lies ahead might keep you from pursuing your true

passions.

Winning Formula:
Welcome uncertainty as a chance to grow and find new opportunities. Take **Rita Moreno**, for example. She's a talented actress and singer who faced many challenges when moving from the stage to movies, especially in an industry that often stereotyped her because of her ethnicity. Even though she didn't know what would happen, she took risks and became a pioneer in Hollywood, winning an Academy Award and achieving EGOT status (Emmy, Grammy, Oscar, and Tony). Rita's journey shows that stepping into the unknown can lead to fantastic success.

Success Hack:
Break your big goals into smaller, actionable steps. This approach helps make the unfamiliar less frightening and gives you a clear roadmap, similar to how Rita tackled new challenges.

Simple Power Moves to Overcome Challenges

Mindset Shift:

Power Move:
Develop a growth mindset, believing you can improve and achieve your goals with effort and determination. Research shows that people with this mindset are more adaptable and successful when facing challenges.

For example, **Alex Scott** started the Alex's Lemonade Stand Foundation to fund childhood cancer research after battling cancer herself. Her dedication and belief in her cause turned a personal challenge into a widespread movement, showing how a positive mindset can lead to extraordinary outcomes.

Building a Support Network

Power Move:
Surround yourself with people who believe in your goals and can offer support and advice. It could include mentors, friends, family, or colleagues.

Zendaya, the celebrated actress and singer, credits her success to her supportive family and mentors who have supported and guided her throughout her career. Their encouragement and advice have been essential in her journey to stardom.

Continuous Learning

Power Move:
Keep up with industry trends and always find ways to expand your skills. Staying curious and adaptable helps you stay ready for new opportunities.

Consider **Iman Vellani**, a young actor known for her role in Ms. Marvel. At a young age, she learned various new skills, such as acting and production. Her commitment to continuous learning helped her enter the entertainment industry and gain global recognition.

Visualization:

Power Move:
Picture yourself reaching your goals and imagine your steps to get there. It can keep you motivated and on the right path. Many successful people use visualization to boost their confidence and focus.

For example, Olympic gymnast **Simone Biles** visualizes her routines before performing them. This mental practice helps her stay sharp and confident, leading to remarkable sports success.

Time Management:

Power Move:
Prioritize your tasks and manage your time wisely. It will steadily bring you closer to achieving your goals.

Think of **Serena Williams**. Her ability to balance intense training with her off-court responsibilities is an excellent example of how effective time management can lead to success. She's excelled in her career while exploring other interests, like fashion and business.

Remember, your dream career isn't just a possibility; It's something you can achieve. With the right mindset, tools, and strategies, you can overcome any challenge that comes your way.

Take the inspiring story of Arunima Sinha, the first female amputee to climb Mount Everest. After losing her leg in an accident, she faced significant challenges, such as doubts and physical limits. But with incredible determination and belief in herself, she pushed through and made her dream a reality. Arunima's story shows you can overcome the most challenging challenges and achieve your goals with belief, hard work, and support.

Write down your career goals and the steps you need to take to achieve them. Refer to this list regularly to strengthen your belief in your ability to succeed, as Arunima did by staying focused on her goals.

By understanding the challenges ahead and using the power moves we've discussed, you can break down the barriers to your dream career. The road may be challenging, but it's achievable. You can reach the career you've always wanted with intelligent planning, persistence, and a positive attitude. Your future is in your hands, so start taking those steps now.

This chapter has given you practical strategies for tackling common hurdles that might stand in the way of your dream career. As you move forward, keep these ideas in mind, and remember that you have the power to shape your future!

Final Thoughts:
- Embrace failure; every setback is a chance to grow.
- Explore diverse paths to uncover your true passion.
- Share your dreams; open conversations build support.
- Overcome self-doubt; trust your abilities and persist.
- Break goals into steps; celebrate each win on your journey.

FROM GOALS TO GROWTH

"Success is the sum of small efforts, repeated day in and day out."

- Robert Collier

5 FROM GOALS TO GROWTH

"It does not matter how slowly you go as long as you do not stop."

- Confuciusius

As you start applying the success hacks and power moves from this book into action, you'll see progress toward your dream career. This chapter will help you prepare for what's next and prepare you for any small challenges you might face. By expecting these possible hurdles, you will be ready to handle them and keep moving forward.

What Happens When You Start Achieving Results?
It's exciting to start seeing the results of your hard work! Early successes can boost your confidence and push you to keep going. However, this stage can also come with its own set of challenges.

Handling Hopes or Demands:
As you start reaching your goals, you may face higher hopes or demands from yourself and others. It's essential to handle these hopes wisely to avoid feeling stressed.

Think about **Kautilya Pandit**, a talented young person from India known for his vast knowledge of different subjects. Kautilya became famous young, drawing much public and media attention. Despite his achievements, he had to handle the pressure to keep performing while focusing on personal growth and learning.

Balancing Success with Staying Consistent:
Early wins might make you feel unbeatable, but keeping up your effort is essential. It's easy to become lazy or distracted when things are going well.

Think of **Gitanjali Rao**, a young inventor recognized as TIME's Kid of the Year for her fantastic work. Even after success, she kept working hard and focused on her education and inventions. Gitanjali's story shows the importance of staying committed and keeping at it, even when things are going well.

What Will Be the First Hiccups?
You may encounter initial challenges as you implement the success hacks and power moves. It is entirely normal and a natural part of the growth process.

Overcoming Lack of Confidence:
Even with your progress, a lack of confidence can creep in. It's natural to wonder if you're on the right path or can keep your success going.

Think about **Yara Shahidi**, known for her role in Blackish and her activism with Eighteen x 18. Despite her achievements, Yara has had moments of doubting her place in the spotlight and her future impact. Her journey shows that overcoming self-doubt is an essential part of long-term success.

Getting Used to New Routines

As you grow and see success, getting used to new routines and tasks can be challenging. Being open to change is critical to managing these changes well.

Look at **Nuseir Yassin**, the creator of Nas Daily. He began by making daily videos and had to adjust as his audience grew, taking on new tasks and leading a bigger team. His ability to get used to these new tasks while keeping up his content shows the importance of flexibility in handling growth.

What Will Be the Small Hurdles?

As you progress, minor challenges will arise. With the right mindset, you can overcome them, as they are a natural part of the journey.

Handling Problems or Delays:

Problems or delays are a standard part of any journey. While they can be discouraging, they often teach important lessons.

Think of **Emma Gonzalez**, a young activist known for her work after a school shooting. Despite facing many challenges in her activism, she kept going and used her experiences to bring about change. Her strength in handling setbacks shows how challenges can become chances for growth.

Balancing Personal and Work Life:

As your career progresses, balancing personal and work tasks can become more complex. Finding balance is essential to avoid stress and maintain health and happiness.

Take **Liza Koshy**, a social media star and business owner. Even with her busy career, she sets clear limits between work and personal life to ensure she has time to relax and take care of herself. Her success in managing both parts of her life shows how important balance is for long-term success and happiness.

Understanding and preparing for these possible challenges is essential as you move forward. Knowing these issues will prepare you to handle them and keep moving toward your dream career.

In the upcoming chapters, we'll explore helpful power moves and success hacks to help you manage your hopes, overcome a lack of confidence, get used to new routines, and balance your life. These tips will turn challenges into chances to grow.

Every success story has its ups and downs. The key is staying focused, adapting to changes, and pushing forward. Your dream career is within reach, and with the right mindset and plans, you can handle any challenges that come your way. Let's explore the winning intentions that will guide you toward success.

Final Thoughts:
- Acknowledge your successes while staying consistent.
- Be flexible and open to new routines as you grow.
- Use moments of doubt as motivation to persevere.
- Aim for harmony between your personal and professional life.
- View challenges as opportunities for growth and learning.

THE CHALLENGING LANDSCAPE OF CAREER

"Science knows no country because knowledge belongs to humanity, and is the torch which illuminates the world."

-Louis Pasteur

6 THE CHALLENGING LANDSCAPE OF CAREER

"Dream, dream, dream. Dreams transform into thoughts and thoughts result in action."

-Dr. A.P.J. Abdul Kalam

As you begin your journey to building your dream career in science, let's take a moment to be inspired by Dr. A.P.J. Abdul Kalam, a great leader.

Dr. Kalam's life is a shining example of what persistence and commitment can achieve. His story isn't just about success-It's about pushing through difficulties with hard work, strong will, and an apparent belief in his dreams.

Growing up in a small town in Rameswaram, India, Dr. Kalam faced many difficulties. But his passion for science kept him going, even when times were tough. Despite money problems and other challenges, he never gave up. His strong will helped him become a well-known scientist, playing an important role in developing India's missile program and leading nuclear tests in 1998.

Dr. Kalam's story shows us that no matter where we start, we can achieve great things with hard work and a clear goal. His life inspires us to dream big, work hard, and believe in our ability to create a successful career in science.

Inspired by Dr. Kalam's life, aspiring scientists learn to dream big, work hard, and overcome any difficulties that may come their way.

As the world of science changes, new opportunities are opening up, and traditional career paths are evolving. This chapter will explore how developments in technology and research create new possibilities for those passionate about science.

Success in this new world requires more than just knowledge; it demands flexibility, a willingness to learn across fields, and an awareness of our moral problems. Let's explore the exciting opportunities waiting for you as you start your journey in science.

Interdisciplinary Approach:
As we move through the fast-changing world of science, the boundaries between different fields are becoming less distinct. In today's job market, roles in science increasingly require a mix of skills from multiple areas, such as bioinformatics, nanotechnology, and neuro-engineering.

Those who can mix knowledge from different fields will be in high demand. This interdisciplinary approach opens up exciting career opportunities and allows new ideas to solve challenging problems. Adopting this trend will help you stay ahead and significantly impact science.

Environmental Protection and Focus:
With climate change and environmental issues becoming more serious, there's a growing need for careers focused on protecting the environment. More and more jobs are opening in areas like safeguarding natural resources, predicting climate changes, and sustainable farming.

As the need to solve these problems grows, the job market is expanding in these fields. There's an increasing need for dedicated professionals passionate about creating a greener, more sustainable future.

Healthcare and Biomedicine:
The future looks bright if you're interested in medical science research, bioengineering, healthcare technology, or genetic counselling. Genetic studies and biotechnology advances are changing the healthcare field, creating exciting career opportunities in these areas.

Ethical Considerations:
As science makes discoveries, moral rules become more important. Careers in bioethics, ethical research, and science policy are growing to ensure that scientific progress stays within ethical limits.

Online Work and Teamwork:
The pandemic made online work more common, and It's not going away. In the future, science jobs will include more remote work, online meetings, and teamwork. Being flexible

and a good communicator online will be very important.
Data Science and Analysis:

Big data has changed science. Data scientists who use data analysis and artificial intelligence to interpret and make sense of vast amounts of information are now in high demand. Their work is making a significant impact on healthcare, the environment, and more.

AI and Robotics:

AI and robotics are changing the game in science and many other industries. Jobs are booming in creating intelligent systems, designing robots, and using AI learning to solve complex problems. This technology is making a difference in healthcare, manufacturing, and space exploration.

These trends show just how exciting and rapidly changing the world of science is. To succeed in this ever-evolving industry, you must adopt lifelong learning and stay adaptable. Let's explore and discover the future of science careers together.

Now that you have a glimpse of the evolving science landscape, it's time to uncover the key strategies to help turn your dream career into a reality.

Final Thoughts:
- Dream big and let your ambitions drive your actions toward a rewarding career in science.
- Embrace challenges as stepping stones to success, just like Dr. Kalam did in his journey.
- Adaptability and an interdisciplinary approach will open doors to exciting career opportunities.
- Passion for environmental protection and healthcare can lead to impactful careers in a changing world.
- Lifelong learning and flexibility are essential to excel in the ever-evolving landscape of science.

THE SUCCESS MANTRAS

"The future belongs to those who believe in the beauty of their dreams."

-Eleanor Roosevelt

7 THE SUCCESS MANTRAS

"When you really desire something from the heart and soul, all the universe conspires you to achieve it."

-Paulo Coelho, The Alchemist

This quote shows that when you passionately follow your dreams, the universe opens doors to help you succeed. Before we find answers, let's take a moment to understand where you are on your journey. You've examined the myths and truths about science careers and are ready to shape your future.

Now, let's discuss the plan- a straightforward way to reach your dream career. Think of it as a roadmap guiding you every step of the way. This chapter introduces a simple but solid 7-step mantra to help you get from where you are now to where you want to be. It isn't just an idea- it's a proven way that has worked for many and can work for you, too.

As we examine each step, I'll share examples and stories to show how others have used this approach to succeed. By the end of this chapter, you'll understand how to turn your dreams into reality.

Discover a Strong Seven-Step Success Mantra:
Why focus on the number 7? There's something special about this number. It represents the seven continents and wonders of the world, as well as the seven days of the week and the seven colours of the rainbow. Even in Indian mythology, the "Saptarshi constellation" has seven stars. 7 holds a special place in history, traditions, and our minds.

So, welcome this idea. Start listening to your inner voice; you might be surprised by the positive changes it brings to your journey toward success.

Consider **Amanda Gorman**, the young poet who wowed the world with her poem "The Hill We Climb" at the 2021 U.S. Presidential Inauguration. Even though she faced problems like a speech issue, Amanda believed in her ability and followed her love for poetry. Her hard work led her to inspire millions and become a symbol of young creativity and bravery.

This example shows how trusting yourself can lead to outstanding achievements. When you listen to your inner voice, you find strengths that push you forward. On your career journey, this self-belief can lead to significant achievements and a satisfying path to success.

Find Your Career Path:
Start by looking at what interests you and what you care about. If you love helping others, giving advice or working in

healthcare might be a good fit. Environmental science could match your values if you care about protecting the environment. If you're good at solving problems, technology or engineering might be the right field.

Think of your career as a painting that shows your passions. Look at your unique skills and strengths. Turn your dreams into a clear plan. For example, if you want to start your own business, outline steps like market research and growth to make it happen.

Action Steps:
- List what interests you.
- Find your strengths.
- Create a step-by-step plan for your career goals.

Exploring New Career Paths:
Try new activities to see what you like. It's like opening a door to new chances. For example, take a cooking class or explore digital art to find what you enjoy.

Be curious and examine different subjects. Like a detective, explore areas you know little about, such as marine biology or creative writing. You might discover a hidden skill or passion.

Imagine your career as an exciting adventure. Every new experience is like exploring unknown places. Each step can lead to fun discoveries, whether a new hobby or a different class.

Look for chances where you might not expect them. Attend workshops or join online groups to learn about new career paths or projects.

Welcome surprises and challenges-they make your career journey more fun. If a new project comes up, take it on with energy. It could lead to surprising achievements.

Action Steps:
- Try new activities.
- Explore different subjects.
- Stay open to new chances.

Connecting and Mentoring:

Think of industry events as your unique access to a helpful community. Instead of seeing them as a burden, view them as chances to meet people who can support you along your journey.

Find mentors who have experience considerable and share insights that match your goals. These mentors are like guides who understand your journey and can offer helpful advice.

Remember, mentoring doesn't have to be formal. It can be simple talks and advice that feel real and helpful. Let their guidance light up your career path in valuable ways.

Action Steps:
- Attend industry events with an open mind.
- Find mentors who fit your goals.
- Have meaningful conversations.

Unleashing the Power of Learning and Tech Wonders
Think of your career journey as an exciting adventure. Every new experience is a chance to learn and grow, filling your path with discovery and joy. Welcome learning and see every change as an exciting lesson.

Explore interesting fields like AI, Biotechnology, and Data Science with energy. Use AI tools to make your work easier and faster and keep up with the latest tech trends.
Technology improves your skills and opens up new opportunities.

Action Steps:
- Take advantage of new learning opportunities.
- Use technology.
- Keep up with industry trends to stay ahead.

Research Tools and Global Collaborations:
Think of research tools as your superhero toolkit. Like superheroes use special tools, scientists use microscopes to reveal tiny details and find hidden parts of their experiments. For example, using a DNA tester helps unlock the secrets of genetics.

Working with scientists from around the world is like joining a superhero team. Each researcher brings unique skills and ideas, making it easier to solve science problems.

Working with a global team has significant benefits, like different views and skills. While working across different time zones can be challenging, the shared knowledge from a worldwide network can help your research and career.

Action Steps:
- Use advanced research tools.
- Look for global collaborations.
- Manage time zone challenges well.

Skill Development for Life:
Building skills is like taking small steps on your journey. Start by figuring out which specific skills you need for your field. Focusing on social media management or data analysis can be very helpful in marketing.

Think of your skills as tools for success. Learning programming languages like Python can make you more valuable and open up new technological chances.

Gaining new skills boosts your career. Each skill you learn has clear benefits, like improving your project management or leadership abilities. By continually improving your skills, you become an essential member of your organization.

Action Steps:
- Identify critical skills for your field.
- Work on developing them.
- Apply them to improve your career.

Digital Age and Power of Technology:
Think of computer skills as powerful tools that help you stay at the cutting edge of research. Using data analysis software makes managing and knowing large datasets easier. Welcome the digital age with enthusiasm. Digital tools can help you do virtual experiments and test situations, speeding up the research process.

Action Steps:
- Master digital tools.
- Stay updated with technology.
- Use technology to improve your research.

Each success strategy is a powerful tool for turning your career dreams into reality. In the upcoming chapters, we'll explore ideas, skills, and mindsets to help you master each strategy. Get ready to take tangible steps toward shaping your dream career.

Final Thoughts:
- Follow your passions-they guide you to a successful science career.
- New experiences reveal hidden talents and spark interests.
- Seek mentors and build connections for guidance on your journey.
- Embrace lifelong learning and technology to stay relevant and open new opportunities.
- Act with confidence, every step brings you closer to your dream in the evolving world of science.

DISCOVER YOUR CAREER PATH

"You are never too old to set another goal or to dream a new dream."

- C.S. Lewis.

8 DISCOVER YOUR CAREER PATH

"The biggest adventure you can take is to live the life of your dreams."

- Oprah Winfrey

As we move into the heart of each success principle, you'll find the practical steps and changes in your way of thinking needed to make these principles real. Let's explore each one, breaking it down into simple, doable steps to guide you toward your dream career.

Every journey starts with a single step, and the journey toward your dream career is no different. But this journey is unique because it begins with looking inside rather than outside. Finding your career path is not just about finding a job that pays the bills; It's about finding work that makes you feel alive. When your work matches your values, passions, and strengths, it becomes more than just a job- a source of joy, satisfaction, and purpose. The key to finding such a path lies in learning about yourself, exploring options, and building a vision.

Learning About Yourself, the Foundation of Your Career Path:

Learning about yourself is the foundation of a rewarding career. It involves understanding who you are at your core- your interests, values, strengths, and passions. These elements are the building blocks of a career that connects with your true self.

To start this journey of learning about yourself, ask yourself some basic questions:

- What activities make you lose track of time?
- What topics could you talk about for hours?
- What values are important to you?
- What are your natural talents and strengths?

Power Move: Thinking About Yourself

Take time to think about yourself. It may involve writing, meditating, or sitting quietly to think deeply about your experiences.

Reflect on your personal and professional past.
- What did you enjoy most?
- What were your most significant achievements?
- What were the moments when you felt truly alive and involved?
- Write these down, and look for patterns.

These patterns are clues to your core interests and passions.

Power Move: Explore Options

Once you understand your interests and strengths, it's time to explore your options. The world has diverse career paths, many of which you may need to learn about. Use online resources like career quizzes, job boards, and industry blogs to explore different professions. Attend career fairs, webinars, and workshops. Speak to professionals in fields that interest you. Ask them about their daily responsibilities, challenges, and what they love about their work. The more you explore, the better your career decisions will be.

Power Move: Create a Vision
With your new insights, start creating a vision for your career.
- Picture your ideal workday.
- Where are you working?
- What kind of tasks are you doing?
- Who are you working with?
- How do you feel at the end of the day?

Creating a vision helps simplify your career goals and gives you a roadmap. This vision doesn't have to be perfect, or final- it's a starting point from which you can improve over time.

Skills:

Self-Awareness:
Building self-awareness is essential in this process. It's about understanding your strengths, weaknesses, values, and what drives you. Self-awareness helps you make career choices that match your true self.

Research:
Learning how to research different career paths is an important skill. It includes examining information online, connecting with professionals, participating in industry events, and pursuing work experiences or volunteer opportunities to

gain direct experience.

Goal Setting:
Setting clear and achievable goals is essential for turning your vision into reality. Break down your long-term career goals into smaller, doable steps.
For example, if you want to become a graphic designer, your first step might be to take a design course or start a portfolio.

Way of Thinking:
Your way of thinking plays a vital role in this journey. Believe that you have a unique purpose and that your career should reflect it. This belief will give you the courage to follow paths that may not seem familiar or safe. Stay open to exploring new options, even if they initially seem complicated.

Remember, **the most rewarding careers often match your true self, not just what society expectations.**

Consider **Michelle Phan**, a Vietnamese American entrepreneur and beauty influencer known globally. Michelle started by sharing her makeup tutorials on YouTube, a platform she used to show her talent and passion for beauty. Despite early challenges, including doubts about whether a beauty career on YouTube would work, she stayed committed to her vision. She runs a successful beauty business today, showing that pursuing what you love can become a successful career.

Another example is **Shravan** and **Sanjay Kumaran**, teenage app developers from India. These two brothers started experimenting with coding when they were just 12 and 10 years old. Driven by their love for technology, they created multiple apps, some of which became popular worldwide. Their journey wasn't always easy- they faced many challenges and had to learn through trial and error- but their dedication and love for coding helped them succeed. Today, they are celebrated as young tech innovators, proving that you can follow your passion even at a young age.

Let's consider **Patricia Medici**, a conservation biologist from Brazil. Patricia combined her deep love for wildlife and her desire to protect endangered species to build a successful career in conservation. Working in the Amazon, she has protected the tapir, a large mammal on the verge of extinction. By matching her values with her work, Patricia found a career that fulfilled her and significantly impacted the environment.

Finally, **Huda Kattan** is a talented entrepreneur who created the famous beauty brand Huda Beauty. She started as a makeup artist and beauty blogger, sharing her love for makeup on social media. Even though she faced tough challenges in the beauty world, Huda's passion and creativity helped her build a brand many people adore. Today, Huda Beauty is known all over the globe, showing how following your dreams can turn a hobby into a successful business.

These stories show how discovering and following your passion can lead to remarkable success. Whether building a global brand, developing new technologies, protecting wildlife, or cleaning up the oceans, the common thread is a deep match between personal passion and professional work.

Finding your career path is a deeply personal journey that requires deep thinking, exploration, and vision. It's about finding a career that pays the bills and feeds your soul.

By taking the time to understand your true self, exploring different options, and creating a clear vision for your future, you can start a career path that brings you happiness and success.

Remember, **your career is a journey, not a destination, so enjoy the process of finding where it will take you.**

Final Thoughts:
- Understand your interests and values—they're the foundation of your dream career.
- Embrace new experiences to uncover your true path.
- Envision your ideal work-life and let it guide your steps forward.
- Stay open to change; unexpected turns can bring amazing opportunities.
- Pursue what you love, and let your passions lead you to success.

EXPLORING EXCITING CAREER PATHS

"Life is either a daring adventure or nothing at all."

- Helen Keller

9 EXPLORING EXCITING CAREER PATHS

"The only way to do great work is to love what you do. If you haven't found it yet, keep looking. Don't settle."

- Steve Jobs

Now that you've started understanding what interests you, it's time to look into more things. For example, finding your career option and checking out different career choices is a journey. It's not about choosing one right away but about trying out different chances that could lead you to your dream career.

Looking into career options is like starting a new adventure. Every experience is a chance to discover hidden skills and interests you didn't know you had. As you look into different career options, keep an open mind and approach each chance with interest-you might discover something exciting unexpectedly.

Success Tips:

Try New Things:
Step out of your usual routine and try activities you haven't done before, like helping others, getting work experience, or even starting new hobbies. These can help you find interests that might turn into career paths.

Consider **Emma Chamberlain**, a popular YouTuber who didn't start with a clear job plan. She began making videos as a hobby and found her skill in creating content and fashion. By trying something new, she saw a career that perfectly fit her interests and abilities.

Network Actively:
Go to events, join online groups, and connect with experts from different fields. Learning from others' experiences can give you new ideas about job options.

For example, **Ruchi Sanghvi**, the first female engineer at Facebook, didn't always plan to work in tech. She met people in the field and learned about opportunities, which led her to an exciting job in software engineering.

Stay Curious:
Keep learning about different fields. The more you investigate, the more likely you will find something that matches your interests.

Take **Dr Jennifer Doudna**, who helped create CRISPR gene-editing technology. She stayed interested in science throughout her career, and her passion for DNA led her to make discoveries that changed genetics.

Skills:

Be Open to Change:
Being open to change is essential in today's world. You may start by thinking you'll follow one path but do well in something different. Practice being open to change by trying new things and learning from difficulties.

Build this skill:
When faced with something new or challenging, instead of pushing it away, ask yourself, "What can I learn from this?" For instance, **Emma Chamberlain** didn't know where her YouTube videos would take her, but by being open to change and adapting her content, she built a diverse and successful career.

Connecting with Others:
Building relationships with people from different fields can open doors you didn't know existed. Connecting isn't just about asking for help; It's about forming real bonds and learning from others.

Build this skill:
Start by attending local events or joining online groups related to your interests. For example, **Ruchi Sanghvi** met tech experts during her studies, which led her to critical roles at companies like Facebook.

Stay Curious:
Curiosity means wanting to learn and try new things. When you stay curious, you're open to finding new ideas and chances that could guide you toward a career you enjoy.

Build this skill:
Ask questions, look into new topics, and keep an open mind. Like **Dr Jennifer Doudna**, who followed her interest in science, you can explore paths you hadn't thought about before. Read books, watch documentaries, and attend workshops to grow your knowledge.

Mindset:
Your mindset matters when you're exploring career options. Approach this journey with an open mind and believe that the right career is out there for you, even if it takes time. Be willing to take risks and follow your interests, even if the path is unusual.

Dr. Devi Shetty, a heart surgeon from India, started with an interest in medicine. However, his passion for making healthcare available to everyone led him to set up Narayana Health, where he brought new ideas to affordable healthcare. His mindset of helping others and thinking out of the box enabled him to find career opportunities beyond the usual medical path.

Emma Chamberlain took risks by trying something new- making YouTube videos. Her open-minded approach to creating content led her to explore other fields, including podcasting and fashion, and build a career that brings her joy and success.

Dr. Jennifer Doudna followed her love for science with an open mind. She didn't plan to change her focus to genetics but allowed her interest to guide her. Today, her work has changed the future of medicine, showing how exploring can lead to excellent results.

Final Thoughts:
- Embrace curiosity and explore career options with an open mind.
- Step out of your comfort zone to discover hidden talents and interests.
- Build connections to unlock unexpected opportunities.
- Stay flexible; the right path may differ from your initial vision.
- Let your interests guide you—each question can lead to new opportunities and inspiration.

CONNECTING AND MENTORING

"Your network is your net worth."

- Porter Gale

10 CONNECTING AND MENTORING

"Surround yourself with only people who are going to lift you higher."

- Oprah Winfrey

You'll realize you don't have to go through this alone as you explore different career paths. Building connections and finding mentors who can support you is just as important as finding your interests. The right people can help you discover new opportunities, handle difficulties, and reach your goals faster.

Building connections and seeking mentors are critical steps in your career path. A mentor can give you helpful advice, open doors to new opportunities, and help you overcome difficulties. Having a solid group of helpful people around you can significantly increase your chances of success. Let's cover some practical tips, fundamental skills, and the right approach to help you make the most of connecting and mentoring. Remember, the right connections can lift you to greater heights.

Success Tips:

Identify Potential Mentors:
Look for people whose careers motivate you. Reach out to them with a genuine interest in learning from their experiences. A guide doesn't have to be someone you know personally-they can also be someone you look up to from a distance.

Build Real Connections:
Networking isn't just about collecting business cards or having an extended contacts list. Focus on creating meaningful relationships. Attend events, join professional groups, and have genuine conversations where you can both learn and share.

Give Back:
Remember, mentorship works both ways. As you learn from others, also share your knowledge and experiences. By helping others, you create a helpful group that benefits everyone.

Skills:

Communication:
Build strong people skills that allow you to connect clearly with others. Good communication is critical to forming and keeping connections.

Understanding:
Learn to connect with the experiences of your mentors and peers. It helps in creating deeper bonds.

Teamwork:
Work well with others, valuing their ideas and advice. A team-based approach ensures that you grow together with your network.

Mindset:
See networking and mentoring as chances for mutual growth. Be open to learning from others while also sharing your ideas and experiences. This knowledge-sharing will strengthen your network and help you succeed.

Consider the story of **Naomi Osaka**, the young tennis star who became the first Asian player to hold the top ranking in singles. Early in her career, Naomi connected with other tennis professionals and coaches who guided her and helped her improve her game. With their support, she handled the challenges of the professional tennis world. Naomi also became a voice for mental health, sharing her experiences to help others. Her story shows how mentorship and strong connections can help you succeed and how giving back can positively impact others. Building connections and seeking mentorship are practical tools in your career path.

By finding potential mentors, making authentic connections, and contributing, you can create a network that supports your growth. Remember, the right connections can lift you higher and help you achieve your career dreams.

Final Thoughts:
- Explore careers with the help of mentors and supportive connections.
- Focus on building real relationships, not just growing your contact list.
- Find mentors who inspire you and can guide you through challenges.
- Mentorship works both ways—sharing knowledge helps everyone grow.
- Network with an open mind, ready to learn and share.
- Build connections that bring success and hope to everyone involved.

THE POWER OF LEARNING AND TECHNOLOGY

"Education is the most powerful weapon which you can use to change the world."

- Nelson Mandela

11 THE POWER OF LEARNING AND TECHNOLOGY

"Live as if you were to die tomorrow. Learn as if you were to live forever."

- Mahatma Gandhi

In today's rapidly changing world, the ability to learn skill and adapt is more important than ever. Learning isn't just something you do in school-It's a continuous process. Every new skill you gain increases the value of your career and creates opportunities. By adopting learning and staying informed with technology, you can stay ahead.

But how do you keep that improvement going? It's about making learning a routine, staying interested, and using technology as your friend. Let's explore some tips, fundamental skills, and the right attitude to get the most out of learning and technology in your career.

Success Tips:

Adopt Continuous Learning:
Keep looking for opportunities to learn, whether It's through online courses, workshops, or self-study. Make learning a part of your everyday life.
Stay Informed with Technology:

Watch for new developments in technology in your field. Whether It's new software or a new tool, staying informed will help you work more efficiently.

Apply What You Learn:
Don't just gather information-put it into practice. Use what you learn in real-life situations to strengthen and extend your skills.

Skills:

Tech Knowledge:
Keep yourself up to date on the latest technology that's essential to your career. Being skilled with technology is no longer an option-It's a necessity.

Problem-Solving:
Use your knowledge to tackle problems and think creatively. It's not just about knowing information but also about using it effectively.

Self-Discipline:
Stay dedicated to learning and improving. Set goals, stick to them, and make learning a daily practice.

Mindset:
Adopt a growth mindset, believing your skills can improve with effort and hard work. Challenges aren't barriers-they're chances to learn and grow.

As you move forward, remember that learning and adapting are the keys to staying relevant and successful. Every new skill you gain is a step toward a better future, powered by your willingness to grow and the technology at your fingertips.

Think about **Greta Thunberg**, the young climate activist famous globally for her commitment to environmental issues. Greta didn't stop at just learning about climate change; she used her knowledge to make a difference. She strengthened her message using social media and technology, and inspired millions worldwide. Her story shows that when you combine passion with the power of learning and technology, you can make a real impact, no matter how young.

This chapter is just the beginning. By adopting learning and technology, you're setting yourself up for a career that keeps up with the times and grows with them.

Final Thoughts:
- Embrace continuous learning to boost career value.
- Stay updated on technology to enhance adaptability.
- Apply knowledge in real-world situations to grow skills.
- Set clear goals and work consistently to achieve them.
- See challenges as growth opportunities, trusting in persistence.

RESEARCH TOOLS AND GLOBAL COLLABORATIONS

"Collaboration allows us to know more than we are capable of knowing by ourselves."

- Paul Solarz

12 RESEARCH TOOLS AND GLOBAL COLLABORATIONS

"Alone we can do so little; together we can do so much."

- Helen Keller

In today's field of research, collaboration isn't just helpful- it's essential. Working with international teams and using modern research tools can make your work more efficient and productive. By adopting teamwork, you can achieve much more than you could on your own.

Looking back at the last chapter, where we discussed the importance of learning and technology, working together promotes these ideas. When you combine your knowledge and skills with others worldwide, you're not just learning- collaborating, developing new ideas, and expanding what's possible. Look at key tips, essential skills, and the right mindset for research tools and global collaborations in your career.

Success Tips:

Use Modern Tools:
Use the latest research tools and software to boost the accuracy and speed of your work. These tools save time and reveal insights you might otherwise miss.

Work Internationally:
Build a network of collaborators from different countries. Working with people from various parts of the world introduces you to new perspectives and the latest research, helping you stay ahead in your field.

Appreciate Different Opinions:
Understand the value that different viewpoints and skills bring to your work. Combining these various ideas can lead to more creative and holistic results.

Skills:

Teamwork:
Learn how to work effectively with people from different backgrounds and cultures. Good communication and collaboration are essential to successful teamwork.

Research Skills:
Learn the tools and methods that can improve the quality of your research. Being skilled in these areas makes working with others more accessible and productive.

Cultural Understanding:
Be aware of and appreciate the diversity within global teams. Understanding different cultures helps in building

strong, thoughtful, and successful teamwork.

Mindset:
Value working with others and different viewpoints as essential parts of successful research. Be open to learning from others while sharing your knowledge. This thinking enhances your work and promotes new ideas and shared success.

Consider **Ann Makosinski**, a young Canadian inventor who gained recognition for creating an innovative flashlight powered by body heat. Ann collaborated with various scientists and experts to refine her ideas and improve her inventions. Her success shows how working with others and using modern research tools can lead to advancements in solutions to real-world problems.

As you move forward, remember that working with others isn't just about joining forces- it's about growing together. Combining modern tools, global teamwork, and different viewpoints opens the door to discoveries and ideas.

This chapter continues from individual learning and technology use to a more collaborative approach. By using research tools and working with people globally, you're setting yourself up for success that goes beyond boundaries and brings actual change in your field.

Final Thoughts:
- Integrate learning into your daily routine to unlock opportunities.
- Stay updated on developments to work smarter and remain relevant. Use what you learn in real life to strengthen your skills.
- View challenges as growth opportunities; your abilities can improve with effort.
- Use your knowledge and technology to create meaningful change.

SKILL DEVELOPMENT FOR LIFE

"Learning is a treasure that will follow its owner everywhere."

- Chinese Proverb

13 SKILL DEVELOPMENT FOR LIFE

"The only skill that will be important in the 21st century is the skill of learning new skills. Everything else will become obsolete over time."

- Peter Drucker

Building skills isn't something you do just once; It's something you keep working on throughout your life. The more effort you put into enhancing and sharpening your skills, the more adaptable and valuable you become in your career. Adopt this continuous effort, as it can lead to new opportunities and achievements.

Relating this to our earlier discussions about learning and technology, building skills is an essential aspect of those ideas. Just like technology evolves, so should your skills. Keeping up means consistently improving what you can do to meet the needs of a changing world. Let's review helpful tips, core skills, and the right attitude to become a lifelong learner.

Success Tips:

Focus on Key Skills:
Identify the skills that matter most for your job. Look into industry trends to see which skills are in demand and make those your priority in your growth plan.

Practice Often:
Spend regular time practicing and enhancing your skills. Consistency is essential to mastering new abilities and staying sharp.

Ask for Feedback:
Regularly seek feedback from mentors and co-workers. Knowing your strengths and areas for improvement helps you grow and adjust more effectively.

Skills:

Adaptability:
Be open to learning new skills and changing direction when needed. The ability to adjust is essential in a fast-changing job market.

Persistence:
Stay committed to your learning path, even when improvement seems slow. Hard work over time leads to success.

Receiving Input:
Take helpful feedback to make improvements and grow your skills. Being open to feedback is essential for personal and career growth.

Mindset:
Approach skill-building with a growth mindset. Believe that you can continually improve and reach new levels with hard work and commitment. See challenges as opportunities to learn and move forward.

Think about **Kheris Rogers,** a young entrepreneur and fashion designer who started her clothing line, Flexin' In My Complexion, to embrace uniqueness in fashion. Even though she is young, Kheris keeps learning and improving her design, business, and marketing skills. Her ability to grow and learn new things has led to a successful international company, showing how continuous learning can lead to great success and meaningful projects.

As you move forward, remember that building skills is not just about gaining new abilities-it's about staying adaptable and up-to-date. Always working on yourself and maintaining a growth mindset prepares you for success and opens new and exciting opportunities.

This chapter ties into our earlier discussions about learning and technology, emphasizing that building skills is ongoing. Focusing on improving and sharpening your skills ensures that you stay adaptable and valuable throughout your career.

Final Thoughts:
- Every opportunity to learn unlocks your potential.
- Stay open to change and ready to adapt.
- Consistency builds mastery-make it a daily habit.
- View challenges as stepping stones to success.

THE DIGITAL AGE AND TECHNOLOGY WONDERS

"Technology is not just a tool. It can give learners a voice that they may not have had before."

- Sheryl Nussbaum-Beach

14 THE DIGITAL AGE AND TECHNOLOGY WONDERS

"**Technology is best when it brings people together.**"

- Matt Mullenweg

As you start your career, consider technology your secret tool to unlock new opportunities. As the quote says, technology helps connect us, and learning to use it can open up many great career chances. Whether working in physics, chemistry, environmental science, or even biotech, technology can help you achieve things you never thought possible.

The digital world offers exciting opportunities to make your work easier and help you try new ideas. Even though biotech is making significant advancements, every science field can benefit from technology. No matter what area you choose, learning digital tools will help you stay ahead and make a real impact. Let's review some valuable tips, crucial skills, and the right mindset to fully leverage learning and technology in your career.

Simple Tips for Success:

Learn Basic Digital Tools:
Get comfortable with your field's key software and tools, such as data analysis programs, virtual labs, and online teamwork. These tools will make your work easier and help you get faster and better results.

Stay Updated with New Ideas:
Keep learning about the newest trends in digital technology. Even if you don't work in biotech, knowing what's happening can give you new ideas for your work and help you stay ahead.

Try Virtual Experiments:
Use online platforms to run virtual tests and simulations. These platforms let you try out ideas without needing accurate materials, which saves time and helps you explore different possibilities.

Important Skills:

Tech Skills for All Fields:
Regardless of your discipline-chemistry, physics, or biology, knowing how to use digital tools like research software and data analysis programs is essential. Take online classes to improve these skills and practice them in real-life projects.

Thinking Through Problems:
Learn to work with significant information and understand its meaning. Doing projects will help you practice making sense of data and spotting essential patterns that could lead to discoveries.

Be Open to Change:
Be willing to try new tools and methods. Stay curious about new ideas and tools to improve your work; don't be afraid to try them.

Mindset:
Stay excited about learning new things. A positive attitude toward technology will help you succeed in any field. Whether it's new software or biotech innovations, be open to using these tools to improve your work.

Take the example of **Elizabeth Teo**, a young scientist who became well-known for her work in synthetic biology. At just 22 years old, she found a way to create eco-friendly materials using bacteria, showing how technology and biotech can lead to huge success. Elizabeth's story proves that curiosity and new tools can lead to outstanding achievements.

By learning digital tools and staying up-to-date with the latest ideas, you'll be ready to succeed in any science career. Whether running virtual tests, analyzing data, or exploring biotech, these technologies will help you reach your goals. Keep learning, stay curious, and let the digital world lead you to success.

Final Thoughts:
- Use technology to uncover new career opportunities.
- Learn digital tools to boost your skills.
- Explore ideas freely with online simulations.
- Embrace innovative tools for better results.
- Draw inspiration from young achievers using technology for success.

MEDICAL AND HEALTH SCIENCES

"The good physician treats the disease; the great physician treats the patient who has the disease."

- William Osler

15 MEDICAL AND HEALTH SCIENCES

"Healthcare isn't just about technology; It's about humanity."

-Dr. Ivor Horn

We often picture doctors when we think about medical and health sciences careers. However, there are many other roles in this field that are equally important and impactful. You could become a nurse, physiotherapist, healthcare manager, or medical researcher, just to name a few. The options are vast, and you don't always need to be a doctor to make a big impact.

Consider **Marie Curie**, a famous scientist who made remarkable contributions to Physics and Chemistry. Her work in radiation has saved countless lives, especially in medicine. Curie's journey shows that if you have a passion for science and helping others, you can achieve great things-whether you become a doctor or follow another path in healthcare.

As you think about your path, consider how Marie Curie stayed determined, even when faced with challenges. If you remain passionate and focused, you can overcome challenges and make a difference in medicine and health sciences.

Quick Reflection!
- How do you relate to Marie Curie's journey?
- What challenges have you faced, and how do you plan to overcome them in your healthcare journey?

Modern Pioneers in Medical and Health Sciences:
Let's also look at young professionals today who are making a difference in healthcare. Their stories show that no matter where you come from, you can succeed in this field:

Dr. Noor Al Huda (Jordan)developed an early disease detection tool at 25 that transformed healthcare in her community. Now, she leads a research team focused on medical diagnostics.

Dr. Nia Niazi (Kenya)started a health initiative in rural areas at 28, bringing essential services to thousands. Her work inspires healthcare workers across the country.

Dr Ayesha Khan (India) led vaccination drives in remote villages at 23, significantly improving health outcomes in rural areas.

Dr. Leila Hassan (Egypt)designed affordable prosthetics at 26, helping low-income patients regain mobility.

Dr. Sara Abdul (UAE)pioneered telemedicine at 24, making healthcare accessible in remote areas.

Quick Reflection!
- Which of these pioneers do you relate to the most?
- How can their stories inspire your next step in your healthcare career?
- Growth of Medical Careers:

The demand for healthcare workers is growing fast. The World Health Organization (WHO) estimates a shortage of 18 million healthcare professionals by 2030. Healthcare careers—doctors, nurses, or other medical roles—are in high demand. India's healthcare industry will reach USD 372 billion by 2025.

Careers Abroad:
Healthcare professionals are needed worldwide, not just in India. Countries like the US, UK, and Australia always seek qualified healthcare workers. While you may need to pass exams and meet specific requirements, many opportunities are available globally.

Reflecting on Your Own Medical Journey:
Before choosing a career in medical science, ask yourself these questions:
- Is this the right path for you?
- Do I have a genuine interest in science and helping people?
- Am I ready for the long years of study that some medical fields require?
- Can I handle high-pressure situations and work well under stress?

If you answered "yes" to these questions, then a career in medical science could be the perfect path for you.

The Path Forward:
Choosing a career in Medical and Health Sciences means being at the front line of solving health challenges and improving lives. As you explore this chapter, let the stories and facts inspire you to discover the many exciting opportunities in this field.

Popular Degree Programs:
There are many exciting degree programs in the medical field to explore, each with its unique focus and career opportunities. Let's examine a few of them:

Bachelor of Medicine, Bachelor of Surgery (MBBS)
- Overview: This is the primary path for those aspiring to become doctors. It takes about 5.5 years to complete, including a 1-year internship. The program covers essential medical training, such as anatomy, patient care, and clinical skills.
- Key Focus: Mastering the fundamentals of medicine, ethical patient care, and practical experience.
- Career Opportunities: Doctor, Researcher, Healthcare Administrator, Specialist, Surgeon.
- Real-World Application: MBBS graduates play an important role in diagnosing and treating illnesses, conducting research to improve medical practices, and contributing to public health initiatives.

Bachelor of Science (B.Sc.) in Nursing
- Overview: This 4-year program prepares you for various roles in patient care, from bedside nursing to healthcare management. It includes training in pharmacology and patient-centered care.
- Key Focus: Practical nursing skills, patient care, and healthcare management.

- Career Opportunities: Nurse Educator, Registered Nurse, Nurse Practitioner.
- Real-World Application: Nurses are essential in hospitals and clinics. They provide direct care to patients, coordinate treatment plans, and educate the public on health issues.

Bachelor of Pharmacy (B. Pharm)
- Overview: This four-year degree trains you to work as a pharmacist. It focuses on medication management and patient counselling and covers drug formulation and pharmaceutical sciences.
- Key Focus: Managing medications, drug development, and patient consultation.
- Career Opportunities: Pharmacist, Regulatory Affairs Specialist, Pharmaceutical Researcher.
- Real-World Application: Pharmacists ensure the safe and effective use of medications, contribute to drug development and offer valuable advice on pharmaceutical products.

Bachelor of Science (B.Sc.) in Biomedical Sciences
- Overview: This 3-year program offers a research-based approach to medicine, focusing on lab techniques and scientific analysis to understand health and disease.
- Key Focus: Laboratory techniques, disease research, and scientific analysis.
- Career Opportunities: Medical Writer, Lab Technician, Healthcare Consultant.
- Real-World Application: Biomedical scientists conduct essential research and diagnostic tests that support disease prevention, treatment development, and healthcare developments.

Bachelor of Science (B.Sc.) in Medical Laboratory Science
- Overview: This 3-year program prepares students for diagnostic procedures and sample analysis, playing a pivotal role in disease diagnosis and patient care.
- Key Focus: Clinical lab practices, diagnostic procedures, and data interpretation.
- Career Opportunities: Medical Laboratory Technologist, Clinical Lab Manager, Pathology Assistant.
- Real-World Application: Medical laboratory scientists analyze patient samples to diagnose diseases, monitor health conditions, and guide treatment decisions.

Bachelor of Physiotherapy (B.P.T.)
- Overview: This 4.5-year program, including internships, trains you to help patients recover from injuries and improve mobility through physical therapy.
- Key Focus: Musculoskeletal assessment, rehabilitation techniques, and patient care.
- Career Opportunities: Physical Therapist, Sports Therapist, Rehabilitation Specialist.
- Real-World Application: Physiotherapists aid in injury recovery, manage chronic conditions, and enhance physical function, improving patients' quality of life.

Bachelor of Occupational Therapy (B.O.T.)
- Overview: This 4.5-year program includes a 6-month internship and focuses on helping individuals improve their daily activities through therapeutic practices.
- Key Focus: Occupational therapy techniques, psychological principles, and intervention strategies.
- Career Opportunities: Occupational Therapist, Pediatric Therapist, Mental Health Therapist.

- Real-World Application: Occupational therapists support individuals in developing skills needed for daily living and working, enhancing their independence and well-being.

Bachelor of Science (B.Sc.) in Public Health
- Overview: This 3-year program focuses on community health, disease prevention, and health promotion strategies, preparing students to tackle public health challenges.
- Key Focus: Disease prevention, health promotion, and community health assessment.
- Career Opportunities: Public Health Analyst, Epidemiologist, Health Policy Advisor, Health Educator.
- Real-World Application: Public health professionals work on disease prevention programs, health policy development, and community health initiatives, contributing to overall societal well-being.

Bachelor of Science (B.Sc.) in Radiography
- Overview: This three-year program trains students in medical imaging techniques, such as X-rays, CT scans, and M.R.I.s, preparing them for careers as radiographers.
- Key Focus: Medical imaging technology and patient care.
- Career Opportunities: Radiologic Technologist, Radiology Manager, Radiation Therapist.
- Real-World Application: Radiographers perform diagnostic imaging to help diagnose and monitor diseases, guide treatment plans, and improve patient outcomes.

Bachelor of Science (B.Sc.) in Nutrition and Dietetics
- Overview: This 3-year program focuses on food and nutrition science, preparing students to become dietitians or nutritionists who help people maintain a healthy diet.
- Key Focus: Nutritional science, meal planning, and public health.
- Career Opportunities: Dietitian, Nutritionist, Clinical Nutrition Specialist, Food Safety Inspector.
- Real-World Application: Nutritionists and dietitians develop meal plans, offer dietary advice, and work on public health programs to improve nutrition and prevent diet-related diseases.

Quick Reflection!
- Which healthcare field aligns most with your interests and strengths?
- How can your unique skills and passions positively impact that area?

Eligibility for Medical Programs in India & Key Countries:

India:
- Educational Qualifications: You need at least 50% marks in your 10+2 exams with Biology, Chemistry, and Physics as core subjects.
- Entrance Exams: You must pass the National Eligibility cum Entrance Test (NEET). This test assesses your knowledge in Physics, Chemistry, and Biology. The cut-off score varies by institution.

Abroad:
- Educational Qualifications: You need a high school diploma or equivalent with strong grades in Biology, Chemistry, and Physics.
- Entrance Exams: The required exams vary by country:
    - United States: Medical College Admission Test (MCAT), which tests knowledge in biological sciences, physical sciences, and critical thinking.
    - United Kingdom: University Clinical Aptitude Test (UCAT) or Biomedical Admissions Test (BMAT), depending on the university.
    - Australia: Undergraduate Medicine and Health Sciences Admission Test (UMAT) or Graduate Australian Medical School Admissions Test (GAMSAT), depending on the program level.
    - Germany: Generally, no specific entrance exam is required. High school grades and university entrance qualifications determine admission. Some programs might require an assessment test or interview.
    - Canada: Medical College Admission Test (MCAT) is typically required. Some schools may have additional requirements.
- Language Skills: If the program is in English, non-native speakers require proof of English competence.
    - United States: Tests like the International English Language Testing System (IELTS) or Test of English as a Foreign Language (TOEFL).
    - United Kingdom: Generally, accepts IELTS or TOEFL.
    - Australia: IELTS or TOEFL are commonly accepted to prove English competence.
    - Germany: Some programs require IELTS or

TOEFL, but many are taught in German, so you need competence in German.
- Canada: Non-native English speakers commonly require IELTS or TOEFL.

Average Fees in India and Key Countries:

India:
- Government Colleges: Fees are usually affordable, ranging from INR 10,000 to INR 50,000 annually.
- Private Colleges: These can be more expensive, with fees ranging from INR 5 lakhs to INR 25 lakhs per year.

Abroad:
- United States: Tuition fees range from USD 30,000 to USD 60,000 annually.
- United Kingdom: International students usually pay between £20,000 and £40,000 annually.
- Australia: Expect to pay between AUD 40,000 and AUD 80,000 annually.
- Canada: Tuition fees range from CAD 20,000 to CAD 40,000 annually.
- Germany: Public universities offer lower fees, around EUR 1,000 to EUR 3,000 per year, but private institutions can charge much more.

Did You Know?

The United Kingdom is a top choice for medical students due to its world-renowned universities and innovative research facilities. Additionally, countries like Ireland offer accessible medical education with scholarships specifically for international students.

Helpful Tip:

When selecting a medical program abroad, ensure that medical councils recognize the curriculum in your home country. You should also consider factors like clinical training opportunities, residency placements, and the language of instruction.

Funding Your Education:

Are you concerned about the cost of medical education? Many institutions in Europe and the United States offer scholarships and grants for international medical students.

Additionally, some countries, like the UK and New Zealand, allow medical students to work part-time, which allows them to manage living expenses. (For more details, Refer to the resources section at the end of the book.)

Scope and Job Prospects:

India:
- Growing Demand: The healthcare sector is booming! With a rising need for doctors, nurses, and health professionals, opportunities are expanding rapidly, especially in pharmaceuticals and healthcare services.
- Diverse Opportunities: Imagine yourself succeeding in medical practice, contributing to innovative research, managing healthcare facilities, or teaching the next generation of medical professionals. The possibilities are endless.
- Top Employers: You could work with top-tier hospitals, renowned pharmaceutical companies, or renowned research institutions.
- Salary Trends: Starting salaries typically range from INR 3 lakhs to INR 6 lakhs, but with experience, you

could see growth up to INR 25 lakhs or more.

Abroad:
- Growing Demand: Globally, there's an ever-increasing need for professionals in biotechnology, pharmaceuticals, and healthcare management. The thrill of working with advanced technologies or solving complex healthcare challenges increases the demand for your skills.
- Diverse Opportunities: Think about the exciting possibilities of leading global research projects, managing international healthcare teams, or playing a key role in shaping the future of healthcare leadership.
- Top Employers: Imagine yourself working with global biotechnology firms, leading pharmaceutical companies, or international healthcare organizations at the forefront of innovation.
- Salary Trends: Entry-level salaries start at around USD 40,000 to USD 70,000, but as you progress in your career, you can look at salaries upwards of USD 1,50,000+.

Quick Reflection!
Did you know that today's most sought-after skills in the healthcare industry include data analysis, telemedicine expertise, and biotechnology innovations?

These skills are shaping the future of healthcare and can put you ahead in your career!

Top Hiring Companies in India and Key Countries:
These leading companies are at the forefront of research and development in healthcare, constantly seeking skilled professionals for diverse roles. Whether in labs, business operations, or IT, you'll find exciting opportunities to promote innovation and advance medical science.

Apollo Hospitals:
- Location: All across India
- Specialization: Healthcare and Hospital Services
- Job Titles: Medical Practitioner, Specialist, Researcher, Administrator
- Website: https://www.apollohospitals.com

Fortis Healthcare:
- Location: Multiple cities in India
- Specialization: Healthcare and Medical Services
- Job Titles: Medical Professional, Nurse, Technician
- Website: https://www.fortishealthcare.com

Dr. Reddy's Laboratories:
- Location: Hyderabad, India
- Specialization: Pharmaceutical Research, Development, Manufacturing, Sales
- Job Titles: Researcher, Developer, Sales Representative
- Website: https://www.drreddys.com

Cipla:
- Location: Mumbai, India
- Specialization: Pharmaceutical Research, Manufacturing, Sales
- Job Titles: Researcher, Manufacturing Specialist, Sales Representative
- Website: https://www.cipla.com

Max Healthcare:
- Location: Multiple locations across India
- Specialization: Healthcare and Hospital Services
- Job Titles: Medical Professional, Nurse, Technician, Administrator
- Website: https://www.maxhealthcare.in

Johnson & Johnson:
- Location: Global Presence
- Specialization: Healthcare, Medical Devices, Pharmaceuticals
- Job Titles: Researcher, Developer, Sales Representative
- Website: https://www.jnj.com

Pfizer:
- Location: Global Presence
- Specialization: Pharmaceutical Research, Development, Manufacturing
- Job Titles: Researcher, Developer, Manufacturing Specialist
- Website: https://www.pfizer.com

Novartis:
- Location: Global Presence
- Specialization: Pharmaceutical Research, Development, Manufacturing
- Job Titles: Researcher, Developer, Sales Representative
- Website: https://www.novartis.com

GlaxoSmithKline (GSK):
- Location: Global Presence
- Specialization: Pharmaceutical Research, Development, Manufacturing
- Job Titles: Researcher, Developer, Manufacturing Specialist
- Website: https://www.gsk.com

Merck & Co.:
- Location: Global Presence
- Specialization: Pharmaceutical Research, Development, Manufacturing

- Job Titles: Researcher, Developer, Sales Representative
- Website: https://www.merck.com

They offer dynamic work environments where you can contribute to innovative discoveries and make a real impact on global health. Explore their careers pages for roles that match your skills and goals.

Exploring Career Options in India and Key Countries:

The medical and health sciences field offers a variety of exciting career paths, each with its salary range and responsibilities.

Medical Practitioner or Physician:
- Responsibilities: Diagnose and treat health issues, prescribe medications, and provide preventive care.
- Salary: In India, starting salaries range from INR 5 to 10 lakhs annually. Experienced doctors can earn INR 10 lakhs to crores. Abroad, salaries range from USD 150k to USD 400k annually.

Surgeon:
- Responsibilities: Perform complex surgeries, collaborate with medical teams, and ensure patient well-being.
- Salary: In India, surgeons earn between INR 12 lakhs and INR 50 lakhs or more annually. Overseas, expect USD 250k to USD 600k annually.

Specialist (e.g., Cardiologist, Neurologist, Oncologist):
- Responsibilities: Diagnose and treat specialized conditions like heart disease or cancer.
- Salary: In India, specialists earn around INR 25 lakhs or more. Abroad, salaries range from USD 200k to USD 500k annually.

Anesthesiologist:
- Responsibilities: Administer anesthesia, monitor patients during surgery, and ensure their safety.
- Salary: In India, anesthesiologists earn between INR 20 lakhs and INR 50 lakhs annually. Overseas, salaries are USD 300k to USD 500k per year.

Radiologist:
- Responsibilities: Analyse medical images, interpret results, and work with healthcare teams.
- Salary: In India, entry-level radiologists earn INR 6 to 10 lakhs annually, with experienced professionals making INR 15 to 30 lakhs or more. Abroad, radiologists earn between USD 250k and USD 450k annually.

Pathologist:
- Responsibilities: Examine tissues and fluids to diagnose diseases and collaborate with other medical professionals.
- Salary: Pathologists earn between INR 5 lakhs and INR 20 lakhs per year in India. Overseas, salaries are USD 200k to USD 400k annually.

Pharmacist:
- Responsibilities: Dispense medications, educate patients, and manage medication safety.
- Salary: In India, pharmacists earn between INR 2.5 lakhs and INR 6 lakhs annually. Abroad, salaries range from USD 50k to USD 150k annually.

Nurse:
- Responsibilities: Provide patient care, administer medications, and work with healthcare teams.
- Salary: In India, nurses earn between INR 2.5 lakhs and

INR 5 lakhs annually. Salaries can be higher with management roles. Overseas, salaries range from USD 60k to USD 100k annually.

Medical Researcher:
- Responsibilities: Conduct research, publish findings, and stay updated with medical developments.
- Salary: In India, starting salaries range from INR 3 to 6 lakhs per year, with experienced researchers earning up to INR 20 lakhs or more. Abroad, salaries are USD 70k to USD 120k annually.

Public Health Officer:
- Responsibilities: Lead community health programs, develop policies, and work to improve public health.
- Salary: In India, salaries range from INR 3 to 15 lakhs per year, depending on experience. Overseas, expect USD 70k to USD 120k annually.

Healthcare Administrator:
- Responsibilities: Manage healthcare facilities, oversee staff, and ensure smooth operations.
- Salary: In India, salaries range from INR 3 to 15 lakhs or more, depending on experience. Abroad, salaries typically range from USD 80k to USD 150k annually.

The medical and health sciences fields are full of opportunities, with various paths to suit different interests and expertise. Your career success will depend on your specialization and dedication.

Average Salaries in India and Key Countries:
Interested in salaries for careers in Medical and Health Sciences? Here's a snapshot of what you can expect:

India:
- Entry-Level (0-2 years of Experience): INR 3,00,000 to INR 6,00,000 per year
- Mid-Level (2-5 years of Experience): INR 6,00,000 to INR 12,00,000 per year
- Senior-Level (5+ years of Experience): INR 12,00,000 to INR 25,00,000 per year

Abroad:
- Entry-Level (0-2 years of Experience): USD 40,000 to USD 70,000 per year
- Mid-Level (2-5 years of Experience): USD 70,000 to USD 1,00,000 per year
- Senior-Level (5+ years of Experience): USD 1,00,000 to USD 1,50,000+ per year

Salaries can vary depending on experience, specialty, and location.

You can achieve great success and rewarding pay in this field with the right passion and dedication.

Top Universities in India and Key Countries:

India:
- All India Institute of Medical Sciences (AIIMS) New Delhi, www.aiims.edu
- Christian Medical College (CMC), Vellore, www.cmch-vellore.edu
- Armed Forces Medical College (AFMC), Pune, www.afmc.nic.in
- Maulana Azad Medical College (MAMC), New Delhi, www. mamc.delhi.gov.in
- Post Graduate Institute of Medical Education and Research (PGIMER), Chandigarh, pgimer.edu.in

- King George's Medical University (KGMU), Lucknow, www.kgmu.org
- Grant Medical College (GMC), Mumbai, https://ggmcjjh.com
- Jawaharlal Institute of Postgraduate Medical Education and Research (JIPMER), Puducherry, www.jipmer.edu.in
- Seth GS Medical College and KEM Hospital, Mumbai, www.kem.edu
- Bangalore Medical College and Research Institute (BMCRI), Bangalore, https://bmcribengaluru.karnataka.gov.in

Abroad:
- Harvard University, United States, www.harvard.edu
- University of Oxford, United Kingdom, www.ox.ac.uk
- Stanford University, United States, www.stanford.edu
- University of Cambridge, United Kingdom, www.cam.ac.uk
- Johns Hopkins University, United States, www.jhu.edu
- Karolinska Institute, Sweden, www.ki.se
- University of Toronto, Canada, www.utoronto.ca
- University of Melbourne, Australia, www.unimelb.edu.au

Quick Reflection!
Which of these top institutions do you feel aligns with your career goals in healthcare?

These inspiring stories illustrate how young professionals in the medical field are profoundly impacting healthcare. They often start with humble beginnings and overcome significant challenges. Their journeys highlight the dedication, innovation, and compassion that define successful medical careers.

Quick Reflection!
What motivates you to pursue a career in medicine, innovation, helping others, or the challenge of problem-solving?

Let's explore a few examples demonstrating how determination and a passion for helping others can lead to extraordinary achievements.

Dr. Sanduk Ruit, a Nepali ophthalmologist, grew up in a small village in the Himalayas with limited access to healthcare. Despite these challenges, he pursued his passion for medicine.

Dr. Ruit developed an incredible, low-cost cataract surgery technique that has restored the sight of over 100,000 people in developing countries. His dedication to making healthcare accessible has earned him the nickname "God of Sight" in Nepal.

Dr. Radhika Nagpal, a pioneer in medical robotics, hails from India. She pioneered robotics in complex surgeries, enhancing safety and efficiency while revolutionizing how surgeries are performed. Despite the challenges of working in a male-dominated field, her innovative spirit and determination have set a new standard, making her a role model for young professionals in the medical field.

Dr. Dipa Patel, a young healthcare professional from the United Kingdom, is a shining example of courage and commitment. Despite being a newly qualified doctor, she demonstrated heroic efforts during the COVID-19 pandemic. She worked tirelessly on the frontlines, treating patients and helping to manage the immense number of cases. Even at the beginning of her career, her dedication represents the determination and compassion required in the medical field, inspiring others to follow in her footsteps.

These examples showcase the diverse ways young professionals are making significant contributions to the medical field, overcoming challenges, and pushing the boundaries of healthcare.

Quick Reflection!
What qualities are most important for someone looking to succeed in medicine?

Final Thoughts:
- Exciting and rewarding career opportunities.
- Roles include doctors, nurses, and medical researchers.
- Constantly growing and evolving field.
- Rising global demand for healthcare professionals.
- Ideal time to explore this career path.

Quick Reflection!
What step are you ready to take today to move closer to your dream career in medicine?

Your future in medicine starts now-don't wait for the perfect moment; act today and begin your journey toward becoming a game-changer in healthcare!

ENGINEERING AND TECHNOLOGY

"Scientists study the world as it is; engineers create the world that has never been."

- Theodore von Kármán

16 ENGINEERING AND TECHNOLOGY

"If we want to solve a problem, we have to understand it. If we understand it, we can fix it. That is the engineering mindset."

— Boyan Slat

When we think of engineering, we might picture civil engineers building bridges or mechanical engineers working on machines. But engineering is much more than these traditional roles. This chapter will explore many exciting fields within engineering, such as environmental engineering, which focuses on creating sustainable solutions for our planet, and biomedical engineering, which combines technology and healthcare to develop life-saving medical devices. You'll also learn about software engineering, which drives the digital world, and aerospace engineering, which is all about space exploration and aircraft design. Engineering is a vast and innovative field with countless paths to success beyond the conventional ones.

Let me share the story of **Boyan Slat**, a young engineer from the Netherlands. When Boyan was only 18, he noticed the growing plastic pollution problem in our oceans and wanted to do something about it. He started The Ocean Cleanup, a project using unique technology to remove plastic from the oceans. Despite having limited funds and experience, Boyan used his engineering skills to design long floating barriers that collect plastic without harming sea life. His project has already removed tons of plastic from the ocean and inspires young people worldwide to make a difference through technology.

Boyan's story shows that even young people with determination and creativity can solve big problems. With engineering skills and some innovation, you can also make a meaningful impact on the world.

Quick Reflection!
What innovative solution or technology would you like to create to address a problem in your community?

Modern Pioneers in Engineering and Technology:
Let's look at more examples of young engineers from different regions who are working on remarkable projects:

Tunde Salako (Nigeria): Tunde founded Hadiel, a company focused on sustainable energy solutions for rural areas in Africa. His team developed affordable solar-powered devices to provide electricity to off-grid communities, addressing energy poverty and promoting clean energy in regions that need it most.

Suhas Gopinath (India): At 17, Suhas became the world's youngest CEO when he founded Globals Inc., a tech company offering digital solutions for businesses. Suhas advocates using technology to solve real-world problems and helps young entrepreneurs and small businesses with affordable tech solutions.

Ann Makosinski (Canada): At just 15, Ann invented a flashlight powered by body heat, earning recognition at the Google Science Fair. Her innovation shows how young engineers can create sustainable and practical solutions that make a difference.

Mariam Nusrat (Bangladesh): Mariam works on affordable and sustainable water filtration systems for rural areas in Bangladesh. Her projects improve access to clean water using low-cost, locally available materials, demonstrating the impact of engineering on essential community needs.

Nadya Okamoto (United States): Nadya founded PERIOD, a non-profit focused on menstrual health and access to period products. Her work highlights how young innovators can address social issues through creative problem-solving and technology.

These examples reflect the growing opportunities in engineering and technology worldwide. Young engineers are driving positive change and making impactful contributions in various fields.

Quick Reflection!
Which of these young engineers' projects inspires you the most, and why?

Growth of Engineering and Technology Careers:
The demand for engineers and tech professionals is rapidly

increasing as we rely more on new technologies. By 2025, there will be a growing need for jobs in artificial intelligence, robotics, data science, and traditional engineering roles. Careers in software, cybersecurity, renewable energy, and biotechnology are also expanding.

India's tech sector will reach USD 350 billion by 2026. As more cities grow and new technologies emerge, there will be many opportunities in areas like AI, sustainable energy, and IT.

Careers Abroad:
Engineering and tech jobs are in demand worldwide, not just in India. Countries like the US, Germany, and Canada seek skilled workers in software development, cybersecurity, and renewable energy. Working abroad may require meeting specific qualifications and passing exams, but the opportunities are exciting and plentiful.

Reflecting on Your Engineering Journey:
- Is this path right for you? Ask yourself:
- Do I enjoy solving problems and being creative?
- Am I interested in technology and how things work?
- Can I keep learning new things as technology evolves?
- Do I like working on projects that help solve real-world issues?

If you answered "yes" to these questions, engineering and technology might be an excellent choice.

The Path Forward:
Entering the field of engineering and technology is like opening a door to endless opportunities. Whether you are interested in software development, building infrastructure, or

progressing computer technologies, this career path offers countless ways to make a real difference.

So, let's begin on this journey together and explore the exciting possibilities in engineering and technology. These options are more than just degrees-they're your ticket to innovation.

Popular Degree Programs:
These programs teach you how to solve problems and create new solutions using science and technology. They prepare you for careers that build and improve things we use every day.

Mechanical Engineering (B.E., B. Tech)
- Overview: This 4-year program equips students to design, analyze, and build mechanical systems, ranging from everyday devices to complex machinery in various industries. Practical training and projects help students develops hands-on expertise.
- Key Focus: Crafting mechanical systems, driving technological innovation, and solving engineering challenges.
- Career Opportunities: Mechanical Engineer, Product Designer, Automotive Engineer.
- Real-World Application: Mechanical engineers work on designing energy-efficient cars, building robotics, and creating machinery that powers industries, enhancing both productivity and sustainability.

Electrical Engineering (B.E., B. Tech)
- Overview: This four-year program focuses on

generating, transmitting, and managing electrical power and designing electrical systems for various applications.
- Key Focus: Electrical systems, energy management, and power infrastructure.
- Career Opportunities: Electrical Engineer, Renewable Energy Specialist, Electronics Designer.
- Real-World Application: Electrical engineers develop renewable energy solutions, create efficient power grids, and design electronic circuits that power devices in everyday life.

Computer Science (B.E., B. Tech)
- Overview: This 4-year program introduces students to coding, software development, app creation, and cybersecurity. It focuses on problem-solving and technological innovation in the digital field.
- Key Focus: Software development, coding, cybersecurity, and data analysis.
- Career Opportunities: Software Developer, Data Analyst, Cyber Security Analyst, Web Developer.
- Real-World Application: Computer scientists design apps that transform industries, create cybersecurity systems that protect data, and analyze big data to drive business decisions.

Civil Engineering (B.E., B. Tech)
- Overview: This 4-year program prepares students to design and construct essential infrastructure, such as bridges, roads, and buildings, which form the backbone of urban development.
- Key Focus: Infrastructure development, urban planning, and structural engineering.
- Career Opportunities: Civil Engineer, Construction Manager, Urban Planner, Structural Engineer.

- Real-World Application: Civil engineers design and build safe, sustainable structures, from skyscrapers to highways, shaping how people live and travel.

Chemical Engineering (B.E., B. Tech)
- Overview: This 4-year program integrates chemistry, physics, and engineering to transform raw materials into valuable products and sustainable processes.
- Key Focus: Chemical processes, materials synthesis, and industrial chemistry.
- Career Opportunities: Chemical Engineer, Process Engineer, Materials Scientist, Quality Control Analyst.
- Real-World Application: Chemical engineers develop new materials, improve manufacturing processes, and create sustainable solutions for industries like pharmaceuticals and energy.

Aerospace Engineering (B.E., B. Tech)
- Overview: A 4-year course focused on designing aircraft and spacecraft and exploring the frontiers of aerodynamics and space technology.
- Key Focus: Aircraft design, aerodynamics, and space exploration.
- Career Opportunities: Aerospace Engineer, Aircraft Designer, Avionics Engineer, Space Mission Specialist.
- Real-World Application: Aerospace engineers work on designing advanced aircraft, creating space exploration vehicles, and developing technologies that allow humans to explore the outer edges of space.

Electronics and Communication Engineering (B.E., B. Tech)

- Overview: This 4-year program trains students in the technology behind electronic devices and communication systems, focusing on signal processing and network technologies.
- Key Focus: Electronics design, signal processing, and network technologies.
- Career Opportunities: Electronics Engineer, Telecommunications Specialist, Network Engineer, Embedded Systems Developer.
- Real-World Application: Engineers in this field design the communication networks that connect people globally, develop innovative smartphones, and create the electronics that power smart homes and cities.

Biomedical Engineering (B.E., B. Tech)

- Overview: This 4-year program merges healthcare and technology, training students to develop medical devices and technologies that improve patient care and save lives.
- Key Focus: Medical device design, healthcare technology, and biomedical research.
- Career Opportunities: Biomedical Engineer, Clinical Engineer, Medical Device Developer, Healthcare Technology Consultant.
- Real-World Application: Biomedical engineers design life-saving devices such as pacemakers, imaging systems, and prosthetics that improve the quality of life for patients globally.

Industrial Engineering (B.E., B. Tech)

- Overview: A 4-year program focused on optimizing systems and processes to improve industries' efficiency, productivity, and quality.

- Key Focus: Process optimization, supply chain management, and industrial systems.
- Career Opportunities: Industrial Engineer, Operations Manager, Logistics Analyst, Quality Control Specialist.
- Real-World Application: Industrial engineers streamline manufacturing processes, design efficient supply chains, and develop strategies to improve productivity in industries from automotive to healthcare.

Environmental Engineering (B.E., B. Tech)
- Overview: This 4-year program addresses environmental challenges and develops sustainable solutions to protect the planet for future generations.
- Key Focus: Environmental impact assessment, sustainable infrastructure, and water resource management.
- Career Opportunities: Environmental Engineer, Sustainability Consultant, Water Resource Manager, Environmental Policy Analyst.
- Real-World Application: Environmental engineers work on projects like designing green buildings, developing systems to clean contaminated water, and creating policies that promote sustainability and reduce pollution.

Quick Reflection!
- Which engineering or technology program excites you the most?
- How do you see yourself using it in the future?

Eligibility for Engineering Programs in India & Key Countries:

India:
- Educational Qualifications: You need at least 50% marks in your 10+2 exams with Mathematics, Physics, and Chemistry as core subjects.
- Entrance Exams: You must pass the Joint Entrance Examination (JEE) Main or JEE Advanced, depending on the institution. These exams test your knowledge of Mathematics, Physics, and Chemistry. Cut-off scores vary by institution.

Abroad:
- Educational Qualifications: You need a high school diploma or equivalent in Mathematics, Physics, and Chemistry.
- Entrance Exams: The required exams vary by country:
  - United States: Scholastic Assessment Test (SAT) or American College Testing (ACT), which assesses your general academic skills, including mathematics.
  - United Kingdom: A-level exams in Mathematics and Physics or equivalent qualifications; some universities may also consider the Engineering Admissions Assessment (EAA).
  - Australia: Senior Secondary Certificate of Education (SSCE) or equivalent; some universities may require the Undergraduate Medicine and Health Sciences Admission Test (UMAT) or similar.
  - Germany: Generally, universities base admission on high school grades and entrance qualifications, with no specific entrance exam required. Some programs may require an assessment test or interview.

- Canada: SAT or ACT scores may be required, depending on the university. Some schools may have additional requirements.
* Language Skills: Non-native speakers must provide proof of their English competence if the program is taught in English.
    - United States: Tests like the International English Language Testing System (IELTS) or Test of English as a Foreign Language (TOEFL).
    - United Kingdom: Generally, accepts IELTS or TOEFL.
    - Australia: IELTS or TOEFL are commonly accepted to prove English competence.
    - Germany: Some programs require IELTS or TOEFL, but many are taught in German, so you may need competence in German.
    - Canada: Non-native English speakers commonly need IELTS or TOEFL.

Average Fees in India and Key Countries:

The cost of pursuing an engineering degree can vary depending on the country and the type of institution. Here's a breakdown:

India:
* Government Colleges: Engineering programs are generally affordable, with fees ranging from INR 10,000 to INR 1,00,000 per year.
* Private Institutions: They charge higher fees, usually between INR 1 lakh and INR 5 lakhs or more per year.

Abroad:

* United States: Tuition fees typically range from USD 20,000 to USD 50,000 annually.
* United Kingdom: Engineering programs generally cost around GBP 10,000 to GBP 30,000 per year.
* Australia: Expect to pay between AUD 20,000 and

AUD 45,000 annually.
- Canada: Fees usually range from CAD 15,000 to CAD 40,000 annually.
- Germany: Public universities offer low fees, usually around EUR 500 to EUR 3,000 per year, though private institutions may charge more.

Did You Know?
Germany is a leading destination for engineering students, with many universities offering tuition-free education in mechanical, electrical, and civil engineering fields. Singapore and South Korea are also gaining popularity for their innovative programs and strong industry links.

Helpful Tip:
When choosing an engineering program abroad, look for universities with strong ties to the industry and internships or co-op placement opportunities. Consider factors like language requirements, access to labs and technology, and the availability of project-based learning.

Funding Your Education:
Are you worried about funding your engineering studies? Many countries offer scholarships for international students pursuing engineering degrees.

Additionally, countries like Canada and Germany allow students to work part-time, making it easier to manage living expenses while gaining work experience. (For more information, Refer to the resources section at the end of the book.)

Scope and Job Prospects:

India:
- Growing Demand: Engineering and technology are booming!
- With rapid IT, infrastructure, and renewable energy growth, engineers are in high demand across various industries.
- Diverse Opportunities: Imagine entering software development, cybersecurity, or manufacturing roles. The field offers exciting and diverse career paths.
- Top Employers: You could work for major companies like Tata Consultancy Services (TCS), Infosys, or L&T, all of which hire thousands of engineers annually.
- Salary Trends: Starting salaries range from INR 3 to 10 lakhs per annum, with potential growth based on specialization and experience.

Abroad:
- Growing Demand: Tech hubs like the US, Germany, and Japan focus on innovation and green technologies, leading to high demand for skilled engineers.
- Diverse Opportunities: Consider the exciting possibilities in aerospace, AI, renewable energy, and environmental engineering. These innovative fields offer promising job opportunities.
- Top Employers: Imagine yourself at global giants like Google, Tesla, Siemens, or Boeing, which actively recruit engineers worldwide.
- Salary Trends: Average annual salaries range from USD 60,000 to 120,000, depending on the role and location.

Quick Reflection!
Did you know that staying updated with the latest tech trends can open doors to various exciting career paths in engineering?

The opportunities are vast and promising, whether it is innovative projects or working with top tech companies.

Top Hiring Companies in India and Abroad:
Let us look at some top companies offering great careers in engineering and technology. Check out their locations, services, typical job titles, and websites:

Salary Trends: Average annual salaries range from USD 60,000 to 120,000, depending on the role and location.

Quick Reflection!
Did you know that staying updated with the latest tech trends can open doors to various exciting career paths in engineering?

Whether it is innovative projects or working with top tech companies, the opportunities are vast and promising.

Top Hiring Companies in India and Abroad:
Let us look at some top companies offering great careers in engineering and technology. Check out their locations, services, typical job titles, and websites:

Tata Consultancy Services (TCS):
- Location: Mumbai, India
- Specialization: IT Services
- Job Titles: Software Engineer, IT Consultant, Data Analyst, Systems Engineer
- Website: https://www.tcs.com/careers

Infosys:
- Location: Bangalore, India
- Specialization: IT Services
- Job Titles: Software Developer, Business Analyst, Quality Analysts Systems Engineer
- Website: https://www.infosys.com/careers

Wipro:
- Location: Bangalore, India
- Specialization: IT Services
- Job Titles: Software Engineer, Technical Lead, Business Consultant, Network Administrator
- Website: https://www.wipro.com/careers

Larsen & Toubro (L&T):
- Location: Mumbai, India
- Specialization: Engineering and Construction
- Job Titles: Civil Engineer, Project Manager, Structural Designer, Electrical Engineer
- Website: https://www.larsentoubro.com/career

Reliance Industries Limited:
- Location: Mumbai, India
- Specialization: Corporation (Telecommunications, Petrochemicals, Retail, and more)
- Job Titles: Process Engineer, Marketing Manager, Financial Analyst, Research Scientist
- Website: https://www.ril.com/careers

Google:
- Location: United States
- Specialization: Technology and Internet Services
- Job Titles: Software Engineer, Data Scientist, UX Designer, Product Manager
- Website: https://www.google.com/careers

Microsoft:
- Location: United States
- Specialization: Technology and Software
- Job Titles: Software Developer, Cloud Architect,

Cybersecurity Analyst, AI Engineer
- Website: https://www.microsoft.com/en-us/ careers

Apple Inc.:
- Location: United States
- Specialization: Technology and Consumer Electronics
- Job Titles: iOS Developer, Hardware Engineer, User Experience Designer, Retail Specialist
- Website: www.apple.com/jobs

Amazon:
- Location: United States
- Specialization: E-commerce and Technology
- Job Titles: Satisfaction Associate, Data Centre Technician, Software Development Engineer, Operations Manager
- Website: https://www.amazon.jobs

Tesla:
- Location: United States
- Specialization: Automotive and Energy
- Job Titles: Automotive Technician, Energy Advisor, Autopilot Software Engineer, Manufacturing Specialist
- Website: www.tesla.com/careers

These organizations offer a variety of job roles and operate in different regions around the world, creating many exciting career opportunities in engineering and technology.

Exploring Career Options in India and Key Courtiers:
Are you curious about engineering and technology careers? Check out these roles, what they involve, and how much you could earn in India and abroad. Whether you're looking locally or globally, there are plenty of opportunities to explore.

Software Engineer:
- Responsibilities: Design, develop, maintain, and troubleshoot software to meet customer needs and deliver on time.
- Salary Range: Expect between INR 400k and INR 1200k annually in India. Overseas, salaries range from USD 60k to USD 120k, depending on the project and location.

Mechanical Engineer:
- Responsibilities: Analyse and solve problems, design complex systems, and develop machinery and mechanical systems.
- Salary Range: In India, mechanical engineers earn between INR 300k and INR 1000k annually. Internationally, salaries range from USD 55k to USD 95k annually.

Electrical Engineer:
- Responsibilities: Create, develop, and maintain electrical devices and systems across various sectors, including transportation, aerospace, and telecommunications.
- Salary Range: In India, salaries range from INR 350k to INR 1200k. Abroad, they can earn between USD 60k and USD 100k per year.

Civil Engineer:
- Responsibilities: Plan, design, and oversee construction projects, ensuring they meet regulations and safety standards, and manage construction teams.
- Salary Range: Civil engineers earn between INR 300k and INR 1000k annually in India. Overseas, salaries range from USD 55k to USD 90k per year.

Data Scientist:
- Responsibilities: Analyse and interpret data to help businesses make decisions, build machine learning models, and present findings to non-technical audiences.
- Salary Range: Data scientists earn between INR 600k and INR 2000k annually in India. Abroad, they can make between USD 80k and USD 150k annually.

Project Manager:
- Responsibilities: Plan, execute, and close projects, ensuring they are completed on time and within budget. Coordinate team tasks, manage risks, and communicate effectively with stakeholders.
- Salary Range: In India, project managers earn between INR 600k and INR 2000k annually. Internationally, salaries range from USD 70k to USD 130k per year.

Explore these career paths and find the one that sparks your interest. The engineering and technology world are full of opportunities that are just waiting for you.

Exploring Average Salaries in India and Key Countries:
Are you thinking about what you can earn as an engineer? Let's break it down. Salaries can vary depending on your experience, skills, and where you work. Here's a simple overview of what to expect:

India:
- Entry-level positions (0-2 years of Experience): INR 300,000 to INR 600,000 per annum
- Mid-level positions (2-5 years of Experience): INR 600,000 to INR 1,200,000 per annum
- Senior-level positions (5+ years of Experience): INR 1,200,000 to INR 2,500,000 per annum

Abroad:
- Entry-level positions (0-2 years of Experience): USD 50,000 to USD 80,000 per annum
- Mid-level positions (2-5 years of Experience): USD 80,000 to USD 100,000 per annum
- Senior-level positions (5+ years of Experience): USD 100,000 to USD 120,000+ per annum

Remember, these numbers depend on your field, location, and expertise. With the right skills and dedication, there's plenty of room to grow and earn more. Keep pushing forward!

Top Universities in India and Abroad:

India:
- Indian Institute of Technology (IIT), Bombay, www.iitb.ac.in
- Indian Institute of Technology (IIT), Delhi, https://home.iitd.ac.in/
- Indian Institute of Technology (IIT), Madras, www.iitm.ac.in
- Indian Institute of Technology (IIT), Kanpur, www.iitk.ac.in
- Indian Institute of Technology (IIT), Kharagpur, www.iitkgp.ac.in
- Indian Institute of Technology (IIT), Roorkee, www.iitr.ac.in
- Indian Institute of Technology (IIT), Guwahati, www.iitg.ac.in
- National Institute of Technology (NIT), Trichy, www.nitt.edu
- Delhi Technological University (DTU), Delhi, www.dtu.ac.in
- Birla Institute of Technology and Science (BITS), Pilani, www.bits-pilani.ac.in

Abroad:
- Massachusetts Institute of Technology (MIT), United States, www.mit.edu
- Stanford University, United States, www.stanford.edu
- California Institute of Technology (Caltech), United States, www.caltech.edu
- Harvard University, United States, www.harvard.edu
- University of Cambridge, United Kingdom, www.cam.ac.uk
- University of Oxford, United Kingdom, www.ox.ac.uk
- ETH Zurich, Swiss Federal Institute of Technology, Switzerland, www.ethz.ch
- University of California, Berkeley, United States, www.berkeley.edu
- National University of Singapore (NUS), Singapore, www.nus.edu.sg
- Delft University of Technology, Netherlands, www.tudelft.nl

Quick Reflection!
Which of these top institutions aligns with your career goals in engineering and technology?

To understand the impact and potential of a career in engineering and technology, let's look at the inspiring stories of young people who have done incredible things in the field. Their experiences show how creativity and determination can lead to remarkable achievements.

Quick Reflection!
What draws you to engineering-building things, solving problems, or inventing new solutions?

Let's look at examples showing how dedication and a passion for innovation can lead to impressive engineering achievements.

Ritesh Agarwal: At just 19, Ritesh started OYO Rooms, a network of budget hotels. His fresh approach to standardizing and making accommodations affordable has made OYO one of the fastest-growing hotel chains globally. Ritesh's story proves young innovators can shake up industries with tech-savvy ideas.

Kiara Nirghin: As a 16-year-old from South Africa, Kiara developed an incredible biodegradable material to help soil retain water, addressing drought issues. Her award-winning project at the 2016 Google Science Fair demonstrates how young innovators can apply science and engineering to address urgent environmental challenges.

Shivani Siroya: Shivani, founder and CEO of Tala, uses a mobile app to provide microloans to people in developing countries. Her work in financial technology promotes global financial inclusion and shows how young entrepreneurs can solve real-world challenges through innovative solutions.

These stories showcase how young professionals significantly impact engineering and technology through creativity, leadership, and problem-solving.

Quick Reflection!
What skills or traits are essential to making a mark in engineering and technology?

Final Thoughts:
- Engineering and technology offer dynamic, rewarding careers.
- Endless opportunities in fields like engineering, tech innovation, and research.
- The field is constantly evolving with rapid

technological advancements.
- Growing demand for innovative solutions in various industries.
- Ideal time to explore a future in engineering and technology.

Quick Reflection!
What step are you ready to take today to move closer to your dream career in engineering and technology?

Your future in engineering and technology starts now- don't just dream about it; make it happen

PURE SCIENCES

"Science is the best tool we have for understanding the world around us."

- Carl Sagan

17 PURE SCIENCES

"**Imagination is more important than knowledge.**"

-Albert Einstein

Have you ever wondered how advancements in science can change the world? Pure sciences explore the fundamental principles of nature and drive innovation across various fields. In this chapter, we will explore fascinating areas such as biotechnology, which is transforming healthcare; data science, where mathematical skills are applied to solve real-world problems; material science, which is involved in the development of new materials for advanced technologies; and theoretical physics, which aims to unravel the universe's most profound mysteries.

We'll start with the story of **Albert Einstein**; whose incredible work reshaped our understanding of the universe. Born in 1879 in Germany, Einstein's theory of relativity and his famous equation $E=mc^2$ transformed how we perceive space, time, and energy. His discoveries laid the groundwork for innovations such as nuclear energy and GPS, demonstrating the profound impact of pure science.

Einstein's legacy is not just historical; It's a foundation for today's young scientists, who build on his work and push the boundaries of knowledge.

Quick Reflection!
How can Einstein's curiosity and innovative thinking inspire you in your scientific journey?

Modern Pioneers in Pure Sciences
We will explore the achievements of modern pioneers who, like Einstein, make significant developments in their fields.

Eesha Khare (United States): Developed a fast-charging supercapacitor for mobile devices during high school.

Katherine Li (Canada): Progressing quantum computing with innovative algorithms.

Sofia El-Rabih (Lebanon): She created sustainable water purification methods in environmental chemistry.

Jinwoo Kim (South Korea): Providing new insights into quantum entanglement through theoretical physics.

Maria Rodriguez (Argentina): Researching galaxy formation and evolution in astrophysics.

These young scientists exemplify how curiosity and determination can lead to incredible discoveries and innovations. Their work illustrates the vast possibilities within pure sciences and how they can address pressing global challenges.

Quick Reflection!
How can the innovations of these young scientists inspire you to pursue your unique path in the world of pure sciences?

Growth of Pure Science Careers:
The demand for careers in pure sciences is expanding as we seek solutions to major global problems. For example, forecasts indicate that the biotechnology market will reach USD 1.3 trillion by 2025, and environmental science will see an 8% increase in employment opportunities over the next decade.

India aims to generate USD 60 billion from its research and development sectors by 2026, opening up more opportunities in molecular biology, climate science, and materials science.

Careers Abroad:
Pure science careers are also in high demand worldwide. Countries like the US, Switzerland, and Australia are actively seeking experts in biotechnology, environmental science, and materials science. You can access numerous opportunities to advance your career and contribute to innovative research with the right qualifications and exams.

Reflecting on Your Own Scientific Journey:
Reflect on how you might make a difference in the world of science:
- What scientific problems are you passionate about solving?

- How can you contribute to progressing knowledge and technology?

The Path Forward:
Science is a fundamental driver of discovery and progress. In India and worldwide, STEM fields (Science, Technology, Engineering, and Mathematics) flourish due to research developments and technological requirements. Are you ready to explore the mysteries of the universe and make a significant impact in pure sciences?

Popular Degree Programs:
These programs offer incredible opportunities for those passionate about science. Whether you want to uncover the universe's secrets or tackle real-world problems, there's a science program for every dream.

Bachelor of Science (B.Sc.) in Physics
- Overview: This 3-year program explores the core principles of physics, such as mechanics, electromagnetism, and quantum physics, preparing students for diverse roles in research, education, and technology.
- Key Focus: Fundamental physics principles, scientific research, and cosmic phenomena.
- Career Opportunities: Researcher, Physicist, Data Analyst, Science Educator.
- Real-World Application: Physicists contribute to developing innovative technology, from designing spacecraft and medical imaging devices to solving complex problems in energy and materials science.

Bachelor of Science (B.Sc.) in Chemistry
- Overview: This 3-year program covers the study of chemical reactions, compounds, and material properties, equipping students with skills for careers in pharmaceuticals, environmental science, and the chemical industry.
- Key Focus: Organic, inorganic, and physical chemistry, as well as laboratory techniques.
- Career Opportunities: Lab Technician, Chemical Analyst, Chemist, Quality Control Specialist.
- Real-World Application: Chemists are essential in creating new drugs, testing materials, and solving environmental issues by analyzing pollution levels and developing green chemistry solutions.

Bachelor of Science (B.Sc.) in Biology
- Overview: This 3-year program covers genetics, microbiology, and ecology, preparing students for careers in healthcare, biotechnology, and research, with opportunities for further studies.
- Key Focus: Genetics, microbiology, and biochemistry.
- Career Opportunities: Research Assistant, Healthcare Administrator, Clinical Research Coordinator, Science Communicator, Wildlife Biologist.
- Real-World Application: Biologists help advance healthcare by researching diseases, developing new treatments, and working in conservation to protect wildlife and ecosystems.

Bachelor of Science (B.Sc.) in Mathematics
- Overview: A 3-year program that explores algebra, calculus, and statistics, offering strong analytical skills suited for careers in finance, data science, and

teaching.
- Key Focus: Mathematical concepts, problem-solving, and data analysis.
- Career Opportunities: Financial Analyst, Data Scientist, Cryptographer, Algorithm Designer.
- Real-World Application: Mathematicians work in industries like finance to optimize investments or develop algorithms that power technologies like search engines and data encryption.

Bachelor of Science (B.Sc.) in Applied Mathematics
- Overview: This 3-year program applies mathematical theories to practical challenges in engineering, economics, and computer science, preparing students for data analytics and financial modelling careers.
- Key Focus: Applying math to solve real-world problems in various industries.
- Career Opportunities: Financial Analyst, Operations Researcher, Data Scientist, Logistics Manager.
- Real-World Application: Applied mathematicians use their skills to optimize supply chains, model financial markets, and improve decision-making processes in business and engineering.

Bachelor of Science (B.Sc.) in Biotechnology
- Overview: This 3-year program focuses on biological systems and organisms to develop new technologies, particularly in healthcare, agriculture, and research.
- Key Focus: Molecular biology, genetics, and microbiology.
- Career Opportunities: Biotechnologist, Research Scientist, Bioinformatics Specialist, Pharmaceutical

Analyst.
- Real-World Application: Biotechnologists develop genetically modified crops, create new medical treatments, and work on innovations like personalized medicine or biopharmaceuticals.

Bachelor of Science (B.Sc.) in Environmental Science

- Overview: A 3-year program exploring the relationship between humans and the environment, offering skills to develop sustainable solutions to pressing ecological issues.
- Key Focus: Environmental conservation, research, and policy development.
- Career Opportunities: Conservationist, Environmental Scientist, Environmental Consultant, Sustainability Coordinator.
- Real-World Application: Environmental scientists help create policies that protect natural resources, restore ecosystems, and mitigate the effects of climate change through sustainable practices.

Bachelor of Science (B.Sc.) in Astronomy

- Overview: This 3-year program focuses on studying celestial objects and phenomena, equipping students for research or science education careers in astronomy and astrophysics.
- Key Focus: Astrophysics, space exploration, and observational techniques.
- Career Opportunities: Astronomer, Space Researcher, Planetarium Educator, Science Communicator.
- Real-World Application: Astronomers study the universe's mysteries, from black holes to the expansion of galaxies, and contribute to space missions and the development of telescopes.

Bachelor of Science (B.Sc.) in Zoology
- Overview: This 3-year program focuses on studying animal biology, covering topics like animal behaviour, physiology, and evolutionary biology. It prepares students for careers in wildlife conservation, research, and education.
- Key Focus: Animal biology, ecosystems, evolutionary patterns, and behaviour.
- Career Opportunities: Zoologist, Wildlife Biologist, Research Scientist, Conservation Officer, Ecologist.
- Real-World Application: Zoologists work in field research, studying animal populations and their habitats to protect endangered species, or in laboratories, researching animal physiology and genetics.

Bachelor of Science (B.Sc.) in Botany
- Overview: This 3-year program examines plant biology, covering plant physiology, taxonomy, and genetics. Students can pursue careers in agriculture, environmental science, and botanical research.
- Key Focus: Plant biology, taxonomy, genetics, and ecology.
- Career Opportunities: Botanist, Plant Scientist, Ecologist, Agricultural Scientist, Conservationist.
- Real-World Application: Botanists research plant species, contribute to conservation efforts, and develop sustainable agricultural practices to address the challenges of food security and climate change.

Quick Reflection!
What fascinates you the most about the natural world?
How can studying pure science help you explore it further?

Eligibility for Pure Science Programs in India & Key Countries:

India:
- Educational Qualifications: You need at least 50% marks in your 10+2 exams with Mathematics, Physics, and Chemistry for most programs or Biology for programs like Biology or Environmental Science.
- Entrance Exams: Some programs may require specific entrance exams, such as the Joint Entrance Examination (JEE), mainly for particular science disciplines. For general admissions, most programs consider your 10+2 board exam results.

Abroad:
- Educational Qualifications: Depending on the program, you need a high school diploma or equivalent with strong grades in relevant subjects such as Mathematics, Physics, Chemistry, or Biology.
- Entrance Exams: The required exams vary by country.
  - United States: Institutions often require the Scholastic Assessment Test (SAT) or American College Testing (ACT) to assess general academic skills, including relevant sciences.
  - United Kingdom: A-level exams in relevant subjects like Mathematics, Physics, Chemistry, or Biology; some universities may also consider additional assessments or interviews.
  - Australia: Senior Secondary Certificate of Education (SSCE) or equivalent; some universities may have additional requirements or tests depending on the program.
  - Germany: Universities generally do not require a specific entrance exam; admission is given based on high school grades and university entrance qualifications. Some programs may require an

assessment test or interview.
- Canada: Universities may require SAT or ACT scores for specific programs, and some institutions may also set additional requirements.
* Language Skills: If the program is in English, non-native speakers must provide proof of English competence.
  - United States: Tests like the International English Language Testing System (IELTS) or Test of English as a Foreign Language (TOEFL).
  - United Kingdom: Generally, accepts IELTS or TOEFL.
  - Australia: IELTS or TOEFL are commonly accepted to prove English competence.
  - Germany: Some programs require IELTS or TOEFL, but many are taught in German so you may need German competence.
  - Canada: Non-native English speakers are commonly required to take IELTS or TOEFL.

Average Fees in India & Key Countries:

The cost of studying science can vary depending on whether you attend a public or private institution and the country you choose to study in.

India:
* Government Institutions: Tuition fees are generally more affordable, ranging from INR 5,000 to INR 50,000 annually.
* Private Institutions: These tend to charge more, with fees ranging from INR 50,000 to INR 2 lakhs or higher annually.

Abroad:
* United States: Fees for international students range from USD 15,000 to USD 50,000 per year.
* United Kingdom: Tuition can cost around GBP 10,000

to GBP 30,000 annually.
- Australia: Expect to pay between AUD 20,000 and AUD 45,000 annually.
- Canada: Fees typically range from CAD 15,000 to CAD 40,000 annually.
- Germany: Public universities offer low-cost education, with fees ranging from EUR 500 to EUR 3,000 annually.

Did You Know?

France is becoming a hub for physics, chemistry, and mathematics students, offering scholarships and programs taught in English. Japan also offers advanced programs in pure sciences, with access to innovative research facilities and collaborations with top scientists.

Helpful Tip:

When selecting a program in pure sciences, prioritize universities with strong research departments and opportunities for hands-on lab work. Consider the quality of faculty, research funding, and potential collaborations with international institutions.

Funding Your Education:

Are they worried about costs? Many universities in Europe offer scholarships for pure science students, while countries like the Netherlands and Australia provide financial aid and part-time job opportunities for international students. (Refer to the resources section at the end of the book for more details.)

Scope and Job Prospects:
A degree in pure sciences opens up a broad range of exciting career opportunities in India and worldwide.

India:
- Growing Demand: Explore research and teaching with renowned institutions like CSIR, IISERs, and top government agencies such as ISRO and DRDO. The private sector also offers numerous pharmaceuticals, biotechnology, and environmental consulting opportunities.
- Diverse Opportunities: Imagine working on innovative projects or contributing to essential scientific discoveries. The field is rich with diverse career paths.
- Top Employers: You could find yourself at major institutions and companies leading developments in science and technology.
- Salary Trends: The entry-level salaries for pure science graduates typically range from INR 2.5 lakhs to INR 5 lakhs per annum. With experience and advanced qualifications, these salaries can rise to INR 10 lakhs or more.

Abroad:
- Growing Demand: There are many opportunities to work at world-renowned institutions or with organizations like WHO and UNESCO, tackling global challenges and contributing to incredible research.
- Diverse Opportunities: Consider sustainability, environmental science, and innovation roles. These industries offer exciting career options for science graduates.
- Top Employers: Picture yourself working with international organizations and top global institutions

at the forefront of scientific developments.
- Salary Trends: The entry-level salaries generally start around USD 40,000 to USD 65,000 per year. As professionals gain experience, salaries can exceed USD 120,000, offering substantial growth for those in specialized positions.

Quick Reflection!

Did you know that staying engaged with the latest scientific developments and pursuing lifelong learning can open doors to many exciting career paths in the pure sciences?

Whether you're involved in remarkable research or communicating science to the public, the opportunities are vast and full of potential in this ever-evolving field.

Top Hiring Companies in India and Abroad:

Many well-known companies in India and abroad offer exciting job opportunities across various scientific specializations. Each company provides roles suited to different skills and career goals.

Tata Consultancy Services (TCS):
- Location: Various
- Specialization: IT services
- Job Titles: IT Consultant, Software Engineer, Data Analyst, Project Manager
- Website: https://www.tcs.com

Reliance Industries Limited:
- Location: Mumbai
- Specialization: Petrochemicals, energy, and more
- Job Titles: Research Scientist, Petrochemical Engineer, Energy Analyst, Project Manager
- Website: https://www.ril.com

Infosys:
- Location: Across India
- Specialization: IT services, data analysis, IT consulting, etc.
- Job Titles: Data Analyst, IT Consultant, Research Analyst, Software Developer
- Website: https://www.infosys.com

Indian Space Research Organization (ISRO):
- Location: Bengaluru
- Specialization: Space research and satellite technology
- Job Titles: Space Scientist, Satellite Engineer, Researcher, Aerospace Engineer
- Website: https://www.isro.gov.in

Wipro Limited:
- Location: Various
- Specialization: IT services, research and development
- Job Titles: IT Consultant, Software Developer, Research Analyst, Data Scientist
- Website: https://www.wipro.com

Biocon:
- Location: Bengaluru
- Specialization: Biotechnology research and pharmaceuticals
- Job Titles: Biotechnologist, Pharmaceutical Researcher, Laboratory Technician
- Website: https://www.biocon.com

Bharat Heavy Electricals Limited (BHEL):
- Location: New Delhi
- Specialization: Engineering solutions
- Job Titles: Mechanical Engineer, Electrical Engineer,

Project Manager, Research Scientist
- Website: https://www.bhel.com

Sun Pharmaceutical Industries Limited:
- Location: Mumbai
- Specialization: Pharmaceutical research and production
- Job Titles: Pharmaceutical Researcher, Production Manager, Quality Control Analyst
- Website: www.sunpharma.com

Dr. Reddy's Laboratories:
- Location: Hyderabad
- Specialization: Pharmaceutical research and production
- Job Titles: Research Scientist, Pharmaceutical Chemist, Quality Assurance Specialist
- Website: https://www.drreddys.com

National Thermal Power Corporation (NTPC):
- Location: New Delhi
- Specialization: Power generation and energy sector research
- Job Titles: Power Plant Engineer, Energy Analyst, Research Scientist
- Website: https://www.ntpc.co.in

NASA (National Aeronautics and Space Administration):
- Location: United States
- Specialization: Aerospace research
- Job Titles: Aerospace Engineer, Space Scientist, Research Analyst
- Website: https://www.nasa.gov

CERN (European Organization for Nuclear Research):
- Location: Switzerland
- Specialization: Particle physics research
- Job Titles: Particle Physicist, Research Scientist, Engineer
- Website: https://home.cern

Google:
- Location: Global
- Specialization: Technology, research, data analysis, AI, and more
- Job Titles: Software Engineer, Data Analyst, Researcher, AI Specialist
- Website: https://www.google.com

Pfizer Inc.:
- Location: United States
- Specialization: Medication development
- Job Titles: Pharmaceutical Researcher, Drug Development Scientist, Clinical Research Associate
- Website: https://www.pfizer.com

Johnson & Johnson:
- Location: United States
- Specialization: Healthcare innovation
- Job Titles: Healthcare Innovation Specialist, Research Scientist, Product Development Manager
- Website: https://www.jnj.com/

GlaxoSmithKline (GSK):
- Location: United Kingdom
- Specialization: Pharmaceutical research and drug development
- Job titles: Pharmaceutical researcher, Drug Development scientist, Quality assurance analyst

- Website: https://www.gsk.com/

IBM:
- Location: Global
- Specialization: Technology, research, data analysis, AI etc.
- Job titles: Data scientist, Research analyst, Software
- engineer, AI specialist
- Website: https://www.ibm.com/

Novartis International AG:
- Location: Switzerland
- Specialization: Pharmaceutical research and drug development
- Job titles: Pharma researcher, Drug development scientist, Clinical research associate
- Website: https://www.novartis.com/

Roche Holding AG:
- Location: Switzerland
- Specialization: Pharmaceutical research and diagnostics
- Job Titles: Pharmaceutical Researcher, Diagnostics Specialist, Laboratory Technician
- Website: https://www.roche.com

Microsoft Corporation:
- Location: Global
- Specialization: Technology, research, data analysis, AI, and more
- Job Titles: Software Engineer, Data Analyst, Research Scientist, AI Specialist
- Website: https://www.microsoft.com

These companies offer a variety of job opportunities across different specializations. You can visit their websites to explore specific job openings and get more details.

Exploring Career Options in Pure Sciences:

Are you excited about making a real impact with a career in pure sciences? Whether you're interested in research, data analysis, biotechnology, or environmental conservation, there are numerous opportunities to explore. Here's a quick look at some top career options and what you can expect:

Research Scientist:
- Responsibilities: Design experiments, research, and analyze data to advance scientific knowledge.
- Salary: In India, INR 6-12 lakhs per year. Internationally, USD 60k-120k.

Data Analyst:
- Responsibilities: Interpret and analyze data to help organizations make informed decisions.
- Salary: In India, INR 3-8 lakhs per year. Abroad, USD 50k-90k.

Biotechnologist:
- Responsibilities: Develop and improve products and processes in healthcare and agriculture through research and experiments.
- Salary: In India, INR 3.5-9 lakhs per year. Globally, USD 50k-100k.

Pharmaceutical Researcher:
- Responsibilities: Develop and test new medications, analyze data, and advance medical treatments.
- Salary: In India, INR 6-15 lakhs per year. Internationally, USD 60k-120k.

Environmental Scientist:
- Responsibilities: Research environmental issues and develop solutions to address them.
- Salary: In India, INR 4-10 lakhs per year. Abroad, USD 50k-90k.

Mathematician:
- Responsibilities: Create models, solve complex problems, and develop theories used in various industries.
- Salary: In India, INR 5-12 lakhs per year. Internationally, USD 60k-120k.

Physicist:
- Responsibilities: Research to understand the universe's principles, develop theories, and work on applied physics projects.
- Salary: In India, INR 5-12 lakhs per year. Globally, USD 60k-120k.

These roles offer exciting challenges, rewards, continuous learning and growth opportunities. Explore these career paths and see where your passion for science can take you.

Exploring Average Salaries in Pure Sciences:
What could you earn in a pure science career? Here's a breakdown based on your experience and location. Salaries in fields like research, biotechnology, and environmental science can vary, but this will give you a good idea:

India:
- Entry-level (0-2 years of Experience): INR 300,000 to INR 600,000 per year
- Mid-level (2-5 years of Experience): INR 600,000 to INR 1,200,000 per year

- Senior-level (5+ years of Experience): INR 1,200,000 to INR 2,500,000 per year

Abroad:
- Entry-level (0-2 years of Experience): USD 50,000 to USD 80,000 per year
- Mid-level (2-5 years of Experience): USD 80,000 to USD 100,000 per year
- Senior-level (5+ years of Experience): USD 100,000 to USD 120,000+ per year

Salaries can differ depending on your field-research, biotechnology, or environmental science-but with passion and commitment, your career in pure sciences has endless possibilities, Keep exploring.

Top Universities in India and Abroad:

India:
- Indian Institute of Science (IISc), Bengaluru, www.iisc.ac.in
- Tata Institute of Fundamental Research (TIFR), Mumbai, www.tifr.res.in
- University of Delhi, New Delhi, www.du.ac.in
- Indian Statistical Institute (ISI), Kolkata, www.isical.ac.in
- Jawaharlal Nehru University (JNU), New Delhi, www.jnu.ac.in
- Indian Institutes of Technology (IITs), Multiple locations, www.iit.ac.in
- All India Institute of Medical Sciences (AIIMS), New Delhi, www.aiims.edu
- University of Mumbai, Mumbai, www.mu.ac.in
- Banaras Hindu University (BHU), Varanasi, www.bhu.ac.in

- Madras Christian College (MCC), Chennai, www.mcc.edu.in

Abroad:
- Massachusetts Institute of Technology (MIT), United States, www.mit.edu
- Stanford University, United States, www.stanford.edu
- Harvard University, United States, www.harvard.edu
- University of Cambridge, United Kingdom, www.cam.ac.uk
- California Institute of Technology (Caltech), United States, www.caltech.edu
- University of Oxford, United Kingdom, www.ox.ac.uk
- University of California, Berkeley, United States, www.berkeley.edu
- Princeton University, United States, www.princeton.edu
- University of Tokyo, Japan, www.u-tokyo.ac.jp

Attending top universities can set the stage for remarkable achievements in pure sciences.

Quick Reflection!

Which of these top institutions align with your career goals in pure sciences?

To understand the impact and potential of a career in pure sciences, let's explore the inspiring stories that show how young scientists make significant changes. They often start from simple beginnings and face many challenges. Their hard work and creativity highlight what it takes to achieve great things in science.

Quick Reflection!
What excites you about a career in pure sciences- exploring new ideas, solving mysteries, or discovering how things work?

Let's explore examples showing how curiosity and dedication can lead to remarkable discoveries in pure sciences.

Sabrina Gonzalez Pasterski, an American physicist, made headlines at just 24 when she earned her Ph.D. from Harvard University. Her research on high-energy theoretical physics and quantum gravity has pushed the boundaries of our understanding of fundamental particles and forces. Sabrina's story shows how young physicists can make incredible discoveries and real impact.

Sarah Stewart, a passionate young chemist from the U.K., made notable progress in 2021 with her research on sustainable chemical processes. As a PhD candidate, she developed a new method to create biodegradable plastics, helping address the environmental concerns caused by traditional plastics. Her work proves that even as a young scientist, you can find innovative solutions to some of the world's biggest problems.

Akshay Venkatesh, an Australian mathematician, won the renowned Fields Medal in 2018 at the age of 36. His work in number theory and harmonic analysis has transformed our understanding of complex mathematical problems. Akshay's story reminds us that mathematicians can achieve incredible recognition and success, no matter how young they are.

These stories highlight the incredible achievements of young professionals and show how passion and determination can lead to advancements in pure sciences.

Quick Reflection!
- What qualities do you think are essential for success in pure sciences?

- What step are you ready to take today to move closer to your dream career in pure sciences?

Final Thoughts:
- Pure sciences offer exciting and impactful career opportunities.
- This field includes roles like researchers, scientists, and academics.
- It is constantly growing and holds immense potential for the future.
- Pure sciences focus on exploring and understanding the natural world.
- Now is a great time to enter this field and contribute to groundbreaking discoveries.

Quick Reflection!
- What's your story going to be?
- How will your curiosity shape the future?

Take that first step now; discoveries in pure science

RESEARCH AND DEVELOPMENT

"Research is creating new knowledge."

Neil Armstrong

18 RESEARCH AND DEVELOPMENT

"It is essential to think every day."

– Akira Yoshino

When we think of careers in Research and Development (R&D), we might picture lab scientists or researchers working on incredible inventions. But R&D goes far beyond the lab coat. In this chapter, you'll discover the diverse world of R&D, where professionals work on innovative projects across industries.

Whether developing new pharmaceuticals to fight diseases, creating advanced technologies to tackle climate change, or designing innovative products in the tech world, R&D is all about pushing boundaries and finding solutions to real-world problems. It's a field that offers endless possibilities for those who love to explore, experiment, and bring new ideas to life.

Think about how our lives would be without rechargeable batteries powering our devices or electric cars leading us toward a greener planet. **Dr. Akira Yoshino**, a brilliant chemist and engineer from Japan's vibrant city of Osaka, turned this dream into reality.

Dr. Yoshino's tireless dedication transformed lithium-ion batteries, making them more efficient and safer. Today, these batteries power our smartphones, laptops, and electric vehicles, shaping how we live and move toward a more sustainable future. His incredible work earned him the Nobel Prize in Chemistry in 2019, a well-deserved recognition of his outstanding contributions. Dr. Yoshino's legacy inspires us, showing how innovation can improve the world.

The life of a man wholly dedicated to research and Development can inspire the next generation of innovators. His journey is a guiding light for young minds passionate about making scientific advancements. It shows the limitless potential of human curiosity to explore the unknown. His story represents the dreams of all future researchers, fueling their drive to push boundaries and make a lasting impact on society. His story reminds us that research and Development can create a brighter, more sustainable future for everyone.

Quick Reflection!
- What inspires you about Dr. Yoshino's journey?
- How can you apply that inspiration to your career path?

Modern Pioneers in R&D:
Let's explore the achievements of modern R&D pioneers who, through their innovative research, are driving advancements in various fields.

Shruti Sharma (India): Developing new drug formulations to combat antibiotic resistance in pharmaceutical R&D.

Liam O'Connor (Ireland): Leading developments in renewable energy storage technologies, making significant strides in battery efficiency.

Amina Hassan (Nigeria): Pioneering the Development of low-cost diagnostic tools for tropical diseases, transforming healthcare accessibility.

Yuto Tanaka (Japan): Creating innovative robotics systems for medical surgeries, improving accuracy and patient outcomes.

Elena Petrova (Russia): Innovating in nanotechnology for cancer treatment, focusing on targeted drug delivery.

These researchers are transforming their fields, showing how R&D plays an essential role in solving real-world problems and pushing the boundaries of innovation. Their work highlights the importance of collaboration and continuous learning in today's scientific landscape.

Quick Reflection!
How can I embrace collaboration and continuous learning to enhance my impact in my field?

Growth of R&D Careers:
The R&D sector is witnessing significant growth as global industries prioritize innovation and technology. Analysts expect the global R&D market to reach USD 2.4 trillion by 2025, fueled by significant investments in artificial intelligence, renewable energy, pharmaceuticals, and robotics. This surge increases the demand for skilled professionals in research and

Development.

Experts in India predict that advancements in biotechnology, aerospace, healthcare, and clean energy will boost the R&D sector to approximately USD 70 billion by 2026. This growth creates diverse opportunities for those passionate about innovation and technological problem-solving and offers a robust career path in R&D.

Careers Abroad in R&D:

R&D careers are in high demand worldwide. Countries such as Germany, Japan, and South Korea are leading the charge in innovation across industries like automotive technology, pharmaceuticals, and renewable energy. These nations actively seek R&D professionals to contribute to advancing technologies and industrial developments.

With strong qualifications and research experience, you can explore global opportunities in R&D and work on innovative projects that shape the future of technology and innovation.

Reflecting on Your R&D Journey:
Think about how you could make an impact in the world of research and Development:

What global challenges inspire you to find solutions? How can your curiosity and skills help push the boundaries of science and technology?

The Path Forward:
Research and Development (R&D) is essential to innovation and technological advancements. In India and globally, R&D is critical in shaping industries like biotechnology, pharmaceuticals, engineering, and environmental sciences.

With rapid technological developments and the increasing demand for sustainable solutions, R&D is at the forefront of solving some of the world's most pressing challenges. Are you ready to contribute to innovative research and develop solutions that will shape the future of science and technology?

Popular Degree Programs:
These programs are ideal for anyone passionate about innovation and problem-solving. Whether you're eager to develop innovative technology or create solutions for real-world challenges, there's an R&D degree that aligns with your goals. Let's explore some exciting options.

Bachelor of Science (B.Sc.) in Research and Development
- Overview: This 3-year program teaches students to analyse data, research, and develop creative solutions to real-world problems. It's perfect for those curious and want to make a difference through innovation.
- Key Focus: Working with data, managing research projects, and developing new ideas and products.
- Career Opportunities: Graduates can become Data Analysts, Science Writers, Innovation Managers, or Researchers, helping to promote progress in various industries.
- Real-World Application: Professionals in this field contribute to advancements in technology, medicine, and even everyday products by researching and developing new solutions to global challenges.

Bachelor of Science (B.Sc.) in Applied Research

- Overview: This 3-year program focuses on using research to solve real-world problems. It's ideal for students who want a hands-on approach to finding practical solutions to everyday challenges.
- Key Focus: Problem-solving and applying research skills to real-life situations, making a direct impact.
- Career Opportunities: Graduates can pursue careers as Research Analysts, Applied Researchers, or Policy Analysts, helping organizations and governments make better decisions based on data and research.
- Real-World Application: Applied researchers work on projects that tackle current issues like climate change, public health, and social policies, turning research into real-world solutions.

Bachelor of Science (B.Sc.) in Biotechnology

- Overview: This 3-year program is about using science to develop new products and technologies, especially in genetic engineering and medicine fields. It's perfect for students who want to create innovative solutions in healthcare and beyond.
- Key Focus: Creating biotech products, developing new medicines, and engineering solutions to improve health and the environment.
- Career Opportunities: Graduates can work in Research and Development, become Scientists, or take on roles as Biotechnologists in the pharmaceutical and healthcare industries.
- Real-World Application: Biotechnologists help create life-saving medicines, develop sustainable agricultural practices, and even work on solutions for cleaner energy, making a big difference in improving people's lives.

Bachelor of Engineering (B.E.) in Research and Development Engineering

- Overview: This 4-year program combines engineering with research to help students design and create new products and technologies. It's great for those who want to turn ideas into real, innovative solutions.
- Key Focus: Engineering principles, product design, and research methods to bring new ideas to life.
- Career Opportunities: Graduates can become Research Engineers, Product Designers, or Innovation Specialists, playing a pivotal role in developing innovative products and technologies.
- Real-World Application: R&D Engineers work on creating everything from advanced electronics to eco-friendly technologies, making sure new products are both functional and innovative for everyday use.

Bachelor of Science (B.Sc.) in Computer Science with Research Specialization

- Overview: This 3-year program explores computer science, focusing on research in AI, machine learning, and data science. It's ideal for students who want to transform the future of technology through innovation and research.
- Key Focus: Developing AI, data science, and research skills to accelerate tech developments.
- Career Opportunities: Graduates can work as Software Developers, Data Scientists, or Researchers, helping shape the future of technology and solve complex problems.
- Real-World Application: Professionals in this field contribute to creating innovative technologies like AI assistants, improving data security, and building

intelligent systems that transform industries like healthcare and finance.

Bachelor of Science (B.Sc.) in Chemistry with Research Focus

- Overview: This 3-year program allows students to explore hands-on chemistry research, where they'll conduct experiments and analyse chemical processes. It's perfect for those who enjoy working in labs and want to discover new things in chemistry.
- Key Focus: Lab-based research, performing chemical experiments, and analysing results in areas like organic and analytical chemistry.
- Career Opportunities: Graduates can become analytical scientists, research chemists, or laboratory managers, playing critical roles in industries like pharmaceuticals, food safety, and environmental protection.
- Real-World Application: Chemists with research expertise work on creating new materials, testing chemicals for safety, and developing sustainable solutions for industries, making a real impact on everyday life.

Bachelor of Science (B.Sc.) in Environmental Science with Research Focus

- Overview: This 3-year program is about solving environmental challenges through research and promoting sustainable solutions. It's perfect for students passionate about protecting the planet and finding ways to conserve natural resources.
- Key Focus: Addressing environmental problems, promoting conservation, and developing

sustainability practices to protect the Earth.
- Career Opportunities: Graduates can work as Researchers, Conservation Specialists, or Sustainability Analysts, helping to create a greener, more sustainable future.
- Real-World Application: Environmental scientists are important in tackling climate change, protecting wildlife, and creating eco-friendly technologies that improve our environmental interaction.

Bachelor of Science (B.Sc.) in Mathematics with a Research Focus

- Overview: This 3-year program covers advanced mathematical concepts and statistical analysis, preparing students for research-based roles. It's ideal for those who love solving complex problems using math.
- Key Focus: Advanced mathematics, mathematical modelling, and statistics to tackle real-world challenges.
- Career Opportunities: Graduates can become Research Mathematicians, Data Analysts, or Statisticians, using their skills to analyse data and solve problems in various industries.
- Real-World Application: Mathematicians and statisticians play an essential role in finance, technology, and healthcare by developing models, analysing trends, and making predictions that help drive decisions.

Bachelor of Science (B.Sc.) in Physics with Research Emphasis

- Overview: This 3-year program explores the principles of physics while focusing on research to explore the mysteries of the universe, from quantum mechanics to astrophysics. It's great for students who want to contribute to innovative discoveries in physics.
- Key Focus: Quantum physics, electromagnetism, and experimental and theoretical physics research methodologies.
- Career Opportunities: Graduates can pursue roles as Research Physicists or data Scientists or work in aerospace, energy, or technology industries.
- Real-World Application: Physicists contribute to developments in space exploration, medical technology, and renewable energy, pushing the boundaries of what we know about the universe.

Bachelor of Science (B.Sc.) in Marine Biology with Research Specialization

- Overview: This 3-year program focuses on studying marine ecosystems and conducting research to understand ocean life. It's ideal for students passionate about marine conservation and underwater exploration.
- Key Focus: Marine ecosystems, ocean conservation, and hands-on research in marine biology.
- Career Opportunities: Graduates can work as Marine Researchers, Conservation Biologists, or Environmental Consultants, helping protect ocean habitats.
- Real-World Application: Marine biologists contribute to preserving biodiversity, studying the impacts of climate change on marine life, and

working on conservation projects to save endangered species.

These programs provide an intense research and development foundation and exciting career paths in science.
Quick Reflection!
How do you see your research in any of the R&D programs contributing to solving real-world problems?

Eligibility for Research and Development Programs in India & Key Countries:

India:
- Educational Qualifications: To join R&D courses, you usually need at least 50% marks in your 10+2 exams with subjects like Mathematics, Physics, Chemistry, or Biology, depending on the program.
- Entrance Exams: Some programs may require specific entrance exams. For example, if you're aiming for programs related to engineering research, you should take the Joint Entrance Examination (JEE) Main. But for most programs, admissions are based on your 10+2 board exam scores.

Abroad:
- Educational Qualifications: For most R&D programs abroad, you need a high school diploma (or equivalent) with good grades in subjects like Mathematics, Physics, Chemistry, or Biology-whichever is most relevant to the program you're interested in.
- Entrance Exams: The required exams differ from country to country. Here's a quick look:
  - United States: You might need to take the SAT or ACT, which tests your general academic skills, including the sciences.
  - United Kingdom: You'll need A-level exams in

Mathematics, Physics, Chemistry, or Biology. Some universities may also have interviews or extra tests.
- Australia: You'll need the Senior Secondary Certificate Education (SSCE) or an equivalent qualification. Some universities may have additional requirements.
- Germany: Typically, no specific entrance exam is required. Admissions are given based on your high school grades. Some programs might include an assessment test or an interview.
- Canada: Depending on the university, you might need SAT or ACT scores. There could be additional requirements for specific programs.
- Language Skills: If the program is in English, non-native speakers must provide proof of English competence. The required tests can vary by country:
    - United States: You must take English competence tests like IELTS or TOEFL.
    - United Kingdom: IELTS or TOEFL are generally accepted.
    - Australia: IELTS or TOEFL are commonly required.
    - Germany: Some programs may require IELTS or TOEFL, but if the program is in German, you'll need to demonstrate competence in German.
    - Canada: IELTS or TOEFL are usually required if English isn't your native language.

Average Fees in India & Key Countries:

The cost of studying R&D can vary based on whether you choose a government or private institution and the country where you want to study.

India:
- Government Institutions: These are usually more budget-friendly, with fees ranging from as low as INR 5,000 to INR 50,000 per year.
- Institutions: Private universities charge higher fees, anywhere between INR 1 lakh to INR 4 lakhs (or more) per year.

Abroad:
- United States: The tuition fees for international students range from USD 20,000 to USD 60,000 per year, depending on the university.
- United Kingdom: For R&D programs, fees can range from GBP 15,000 to GBP 35,000 annually.
- Australia: Tuition costs typically range between AUD 25,000 and AUD 45,000 annually.
- Canada: Fees are usually between CAD 18,000 and CAD 40,000 annually.
- Germany: Public universities in Germany offer low-cost education, with fees ranging from EUR 500 to EUR 3,000 per year, making it an attractive option for many students.

Did You Know?

Switzerland is a global leader in research and development (R&D), offering excellent opportunities for biotech, pharmaceuticals, and engineering students. The USA is also known for its R&D programs in renowned institutions like MIT and Stanford, which have strong industry collaborations.

Helpful Tip:

When choosing a destination for R&D studies, consider programs that offer robust research funding and collaborations with industry leaders. Also, look for access to advanced research facilities and opportunities for interdisciplinary learning.

Funding Your Education:
Are you worried about the cost of pursuing R&D? Many countries, such as Canada and Sweden, offer research scholarships and grants.

Some universities also provide paid research assistant positions, allowing you to fund your studies while gaining valuable experience. (Refer to the resources section at the end of the book for more information.)

Scope and Job Prospects:

India:
- Growing Demand: R&D is on the rise in India! With developments in biotechnology, pharmaceuticals, and renewable energy, there's a growing need for skilled researchers and innovators.
- Diverse Opportunities: Imagine exploring careers in drug development, artificial intelligence, or sustainable technologies. The options are endless in R&D, offering exciting and diverse career paths.
- Top Employers: You could work with top organizations like the Indian Space Research Organization (ISRO), Bharat Biotech, or Tata Consultancy Services (TCS), all of which are known for their innovative R&D work.
- Salary Trends: Starting salaries in R&D range from INR 3 to 8 lakhs per annum. Salaries increase as professionals gain experience and expertise.

Abroad:
- Growing Demand: Countries like the US, Germany, and Japan focus on innovation. Fields like biotechnology, artificial intelligence, and green technologies are booming, creating a high demand for R&D experts.

- Diverse Opportunities: Imagine being part of incredible robotics, nanotechnology, or space exploration research. R&D offers thrilling opportunities in advanced areas of science and technology.
- Top Employers: Picture yourself working at global giants like Google, Tesla, Pfizer, or Siemens, where R&D is at the heart of innovation.
- Salary Trends: The average annual salary for R&D professionals ranges from USD 60,000 to USD 120,000, depending on the role and location.

Quick Reflection!

Did you know that staying updated with the latest developments in science and technology can lead to incredible career opportunities in R&D?

Whether you're pushing the boundaries of innovation or working with top global companies, the future of R&D is full of exciting opportunities.

Top Hiring Companies in India and Abroad

Many companies in India and internationally are known for their dedication to innovation and innovative research. Here's a list of some of the leading companies that offer exciting R&D opportunities:

Tata Consultancy Services (TCS):
- Location: TCS has a global presence.
- Job Titles: They offer positions like Software Developer, Business Analyst, and Data Scientist.
- Specialization: TCS excels in IT services and consulting.
- Website: www.tcs.com

Hindustan Unilever Limited (HUL):
- Location: HUL is headquartered in Mumbai, India.
- Job Titles: Roles range from Brand Manager to Supply Chain Analyst.
- Specialization: HUL specializes in consumer goods and personal care products.
- Website: www.hul.co.in

Larsen & Toubro (L&T):
- Location: L&T is based in Mumbai, India.
- Job Titles: They offer positions such as Civil Engineer, Project Manager, and Electrical Designer.
- Specialization: L&T is a major player in engineering and construction.
- Website: www.larsentoubro.com

Infosys:
- Location: Infosys has a global presence.
- Job Titles: Job options include Software Engineer, Data Analyst, and Solution Architect.
- Specialization: Infosys specializes in IT services and consulting.
- Website: www.infosys.com

Reliance Industries Limited:
- Location: Reliance is headquartered in Mumbai, India.
- Job Titles: They offer roles like Financial Analyst, Marketing Manager, and Network Engineer.
- Specialization: Reliance is a corporation with interests in telecommunications, retail, and petrochemicals.
- Website: www.ril.com

Google:
- Location: Google operates globally.
- Job Titles: Positions range from Software Engineer to UX Designer.
- Specialization: Google is renowned for its technology and digital offerings.
- Website: www.google.com/careers

Apple Inc.:
- Location: Apple is headquartered in Cupertino, California.
- Job Titles: Job openings include iOS Developer, Hardware Engineer, and Marketing Specialist.
- Specialization: Apple is known for technological innovation and consumer electronics.
- Website: www.apple.com/jobs

Microsoft:
- Location: Microsoft has a global presence.
- Job Titles: Roles offered encompass Software Development Engineer, Data Scientist, and Cloud Solutions Architect.
- Specialization: Microsoft is a leader in software, cloud services, and hardware.
- Website: www.microsoft.com/en us/jobs

Amazon:
- Location: Amazon operates worldwide.
- Job Titles: Opportunities range from Fulfillment Associate to Software Development Engineer.
- Specialization: Amazon excels in e commerce, cloud computing, and digital streaming.
- Website: www.amazon.jobs

IBM:
- Location: IBM has a global presence.
- Job Titles: They offer positions like AI Developer, Cybersecurity Analyst, and Business Consultant.
- Specialization: IBM is a major player in technology,
- providing solutions in AI, cloud, and IT services.
- Website: www.ibm.com/employment

These companies actively seek out talented graduates for R&D roles, investing in top talent to drive advancements.

Exploring Career Opportunities in Research and Development:

Are you passionate about discovering new ideas and progressing technology? A career in R & D is your perfect fit. Whether you are interested in science, engineering, or innovation, R&D offers many exciting opportunities. Let's look at some top career options and what you can expect.

R&D Scientist:
- Responsibilities: Design experiments, conduct research, and analyse results to drive innovation and knowledge forward.
- Salary: Starting salaries in India range from INR 6 to 12 lakhs annually. Internationally, you could earn anywhere between USD 60,000 and 120,000.

Data Scientist (R&D Focus):
- Responsibilities: Use data to solve complex problems and make recommendations that can influence product development or research outcomes.
- Salary: In India, salaries range from INR 4 to 10 lakhs annually. Globally, salaries range from USD 50,000 to 90,000.

Biotechnology Researcher:
- Responsibilities: Explore and develop new technologies to improve healthcare, agriculture, or environmental sustainability.
- Salary: In India, you can earn between INR 3.5 and 9 lakhs annually. International salaries typically range from USD 50,000 to 100,000.

Pharmaceutical Researcher:
- Responsibilities: Develop new medications, test treatments, and contribute to progressing medical science.
- Salary: In India, salaries range from INR 6 to 15 lakhs annually. Globally, researchers can expect USD 60,000 to 120,000.

Environmental Research Scientist:
- Responsibilities: Study environmental problems and develop solutions for a sustainable future.
- Salary: In India, salaries range from INR 4 to 10 lakhs annually. Internationally, you could earn USD 50,000 to 90,000.

Physicist (R&D):
- Responsibilities: Conduct experiments and research to uncover new insights about the physical world, working in fields like quantum physics or applied technology.
- Salary: In India, salaries range from INR 5 to 12 lakhs annually. Globally, physicists can earn between USD 60,000 to 120,000.

Each of these roles offers exciting challenges and opportunities to innovate. If you're passionate about learning and solving real-world problems, a career in R&D could take you on a fascinating journey.

Average Salaries in Research and Development:

Curious about what you could earn in a pure science career? Let's break it down based on your experience and location. Whether you're looking into research, biotechnology, or environmental science, here's a general idea:

India:
- Entry-level (0-2 years of Experience): INR 400,000 to INR 800,000 per year
- Mid-level (2-5 years of Experience): INR 800,000 to INR 1,500,000 per year
- Senior-level (5+ years of Experience): INR 1,500,000 to INR 3,500,000 per year

Abroad:
- Entry-level (0-2 years of Experience): USD 60,000 to USD 90,000 per year
- Mid-level (2-5 years of Experience): USD 90,000 to USD 120,000 per year
- Senior-level (5+ years of Experience): USD 120,000 to USD 150,000+ per year

R&D roles, especially in biotechnology, pharmaceuticals, and tech, often come with higher salaries due to the focus on developing products, patents, and innovation. These jobs also offer better compensation than academic research positions in pure sciences.

Top Universities in India and Abroad:

India:
- Indian Institute of Technology (IIT) Bombay,

- www.iitb.ac.in
- Indian Institute of Science (IISc) Bangalore, www.iisc.ac.in
- Tata Institute of Fundamental Research (TIFR) Mumbai, www.tifr.res.in
- Jawaharlal Nehru University (JNU) Delhi, www.jnu.ac.in
- National Institute of Technology (NIT) Trichy, www.nitt.edu
- Delhi Technological University (DTU) Delhi, www.dtu.ac.in
- Indian Statistical Institute (ISI) Kolkata, www.isical.ac.in
- Birla Institute of Technology and Science (BITS) Pilani, www.bits-pilani.ac.in
- Anna University Chennai, www.annauniv.edu
- Indian Institute of Science Education and Research (IISER) Pune, www.iiserpune.ac.in

Abroad:
- Massachusetts Institute of Technology (MIT), USA, www.mit.edu
- Stanford University, USA, www.stanford.edu
- University of Cambridge, UK, www.cam.ac.uk
- Harvard University, USA, www.harvard.edu
- ETH Zurich, Switzerland, www.ethz.ch
- California Institute of Technology (Caltech), USA, www.caltech.edu
- Oxford University, UK, www.ox.ac.uk
- University of California, Berkeley, USA, www.berkeley.edu
- University of Toronto, Canada, www.utoronto.ca
- National University of Singapore (NUS), Singapore, www.nus.edu.sg

Quick Reflection!
What will you look for when choosing a top university for R&D studies?

The amazing stories of young researchers in R&D are making a difference. They often start with simple ideas and face challenges along the way. Their hard work and creativity prove that research can genuinely change the world.

Quick Reflection!
What excites you about a career in creating new inventions, solving everyday problems, or discovering new possibilities?

Let's explore some examples that highlight how curiosity and commitment to R&D can lead to incredible discoveries and positive change.

Meet **Lily Thompson**, a young researcher from the U.S. who made waves at just 25 by earning her Ph.D. in materials science. Her work on developing more robust, lighter materials for renewable energy has opened up new possibilities for sustainable technology. Lily's journey shows how young scientists can make a real difference with innovative ideas.

Rajesh Patel, a dedicated young engineer, has been working on intelligent agriculture solutions in India. In 2022, as a master's student, he created a sensor system that helps farmers monitor soil health and optimize water usage. His project highlights how even students can tackle critical issues like food security and resource management.

Emma Zhang, a talented biologist from Canada, received recognition for her research on gene editing in 2023. At only 28, she has made significant progress using CRISPR technology to improve crop resilience against climate change. Emma's achievements remind us that young scientists can drive considerable developments in biology.

These stories celebrate young innovators' impressive achievements, demonstrating that anyone can make incredible contributions to R&D with passion and hard work.

Quick Reflection!
- What skills are essential for thriving in the R&D field?
- What action will you take today to get closer to your dream career in R&D?

Final Thoughts:
- A career in R&D is exciting and impactful.
- You can become a researcher, inventor, or expert in your field.
- It's the perfect time to solve the world's biggest challenges through innovation.

Quick Reflection!
- What will your journey look like?
- How will your curiosity influence the future?

Start taking steps today. Discoveries in R&D are just around the corner!

Your journey into research and development starts now- dare to innovate, challenge the impossible, and become the catalyst for a brighter, more sustainable future!

ESSENTIAL RESOURCES

These resources are excellent tools to help you go beyond what's covered in this book. They offer opportunities to learn more, gain hands-on experience, and move closer to success in your chosen science career.

- Websites for Career Research
- Books for Career Research
- Professional Networks
- Scholarships
- Internships
- Trainings
- Research Grants and Fellowships
- Online Learning Platforms
- Professional Associations and Societies
- Government Initiatives and Programs

Quick Reflection!
- What do I need most right now: career advice, learning opportunities, or professional connections?

- Which of these resources will help me take the next step in my career journey?
-

WEBSITES FOR CAREER RESEARCH

Bureau of Labor Statistics
- What it offers: Get detailed information on different careers, like job duties, education needed, salary ranges, and future job opportunities.
- Website: http://www.bls.gov/ooh
- Reflect: What new career information did you learn here that surprised you?

ONET Online
- What it offers: A detailed look into job roles, skills required, and salary expectations.
- Website: http://www.onetonline.org
- Try this: Use the skills filter-did you find a career you hadn't thought about?

My Next Move
- What it offers: Discover careers by exploring your interests, searching by keyword, or browsing industries.
- Website: http://www.mynextmove.org
- Challenge: Try the career quiz and reflect-are the

results what you expected?

The Muse
- What it offers: Offers career advice, job search tools, and company profiles to help you learn more about different jobs.
- Website: http://www.themuse.com
- Tip: Check out the career advice section-what's one piece of advice you can apply today?

LinkedIn
- What it offers: A professional networking site to connect with experts in your field and explore career opportunities.
- Website: http://www.linkedin.com
- Action step: Create or update your LinkedIn profile. Who can you connect with to learn more about your desired career?

BOOKS FOR CAREER RESEARCH

What Color Is Your Parachute? by Richard N. Bolles
- What it offers: A timeless guide that helps you figure out your interests, skills, and values to find the perfect career path.
- Reflect: How do your skills and values align with your career choice?

The Pathfinder by Nicholas Lore
- What it offers: Practical steps and self-assessment tools to help you find a rewarding career.
- Try this: Use one of the self-assessment exercises. What new career insight did you gain?

Designing Your Life by Bill Burnett and Dave Evans
- What it offers: Helps you apply design-thinking to build a joyful life and career, with exercises and strategies to guide you.
- Action step: Complete one of the exercises in the book-how did it shift your perspective on your career?

What Can You Do with a Science Degree? by Sarah Garland
- What it offers: Explore various career options for science graduates and learn how to make the most of your degree.
- Reflect: Which career path resonated with you, and why?

Quick Reflection!
Learning and career development are lifelong journeys. Which resource will you explore first to get started?

PROFESSIONAL NETWORKS

As you explore career options after high school, joining professional groups and networks can open up many doors. These organizations offer amazing resources like internships, mentorship, and connections with industry experts who can help guide you along your career path. Whether you're interested in medical sciences, engineering, pure sciences, or R&D, these networks can help you discover new opportunities and build relationships with professionals in your field.

- American Association for the Advancement of Science (www.aaas.org)
- American Chemical Society (www.acs.org)
- American Society for Microbiology (www.asm.org)
- Association for Computing Machinery (www.acm.org)
- American Society of Civil Engineers (www.asce.org)
- Association for Women in Science (www.awis.org)

- European Molecular Biology Organization (www.embo.org)
- Federation of American Societies for Experimental Biology (www.faseb.org)
- International Society for Computational Biology (www.iscb.org)
- International Society for Stem Cell Research (www.isscr.org)
- International Society for Optics and Photonics (www.spie.org)
- Institute of Electrical and Electronics Engineers (www.ieee.org)
- American Physical Society (www.aps.org)
- National Academy of Sciences (www.nasonline.org)
- Society for Neuroscience (www.sfn.org)
- American Medical Association (www.ama-assn.org)
- International Federation of Medical Students' Associations (www.ifmsa.org)

These organizations provide great opportunities to attend conferences, read innovative publications, and join mentoring programs. Plus, they offer a chance to connect with others who share your passion and interests. You'll also discover exciting career paths you may not have known about before.

Quick Reflection:
Which of these organizations aligns with your career goals?
- How can you start engaging with one of these networks today?
- Could you attend a conference or explore their internship opportunities?

Why Start Now?
Getting involved in professional networks early on can make a huge impact on your career. You'll gain valuable insights, make important connections, and discover new opportunities that will shape your future. Start exploring these networks today and take the first step toward building your dream career!

SCHOLARSHIP IN INDIA AND ABROAD

This section is here to help you explore scholarships that offer financial support and valuable opportunities for growth. Whether you're interested in Medical and Health Sciences, Engineering and Technology, Pure Sciences, or Research and Development (R&D), there are scholarships available for you. Below, you'll find a list of programs designed for students like you, who have completed their 10+2 education and are passionate about pursuing a career in science.

Scholarships are offered by various organizations, including government bodies, universities, private companies, and research institutions. Each program has different eligibility criteria, application processes, and deadlines, so make sure to visit their official websites for the most up-to-date information.

India:

Kishore Vaigyanik Protsahan Yojana (KVPY)
- Provided by: Department of Science and Technology (DST), Government of India
- Eligibility: For 12th-grade students and those pursuing

Basic Science programs like BSc, BS, MS, or Integrated MS. Ideal for students aiming for careers in research and R&D.
- Application Process: Online application, followed by an aptitude test and interview.
- Deadline: Typically, in August or September.
- Benefits: Scholarships and research grants.
- Website: http://www.kvpy.iisc.ernet.in

National Talent Search Examination (NTSE Scholarship)
- Provided by: National Council of Educational Research and Training (NCERT), Government of India
- Eligibility: Open to Class 10 students from recognized schools across India, including those aiming for careers in Pure Sciences and Engineering.
- Application Process: Three rounds of tests at national and state levels.
- Deadline: Varies by state. Check the official website.
- Benefits: Financial support for higher education and enhanced career opportunities.
- Website: https://ncert.nic.in

Prime Minister's Scholarship Scheme for Central Armed Police Forces and Assam Rifles
- Provided by: Ministry of Home Affairs, Government of India
- Eligibility: Students with a minimum of 60% in their 10+2 exams, whose parents serve in CAPFs or Assam Rifles, pursuing degrees in Engineering, Medical Sciences, or Technology.
- Application Process: Apply through the National Scholarship Portal (NSP).
- Deadline: Varies annually. Visit the NSP website for

updates.
- Benefits: Financial assistance for undergraduate degrees.
- Website: http://www.scholarship.gov.in

Maulana Azad National Scholarship for Girls
- Provided by: Maulana Azad Education Foundation under the Ministry of Minority Affairs
- Eligibility: Minority community girls (Muslims, Christians, Sikhs, Buddhists, Jains, Parsis) scoring at least 55% in 10th-grade exams, especially for students pursuing Medical or Pure Science fields.
- Application Process: Online application.
- Deadline: Varies. Check the official website.
- Benefits: Financial support for overcoming educational barriers.
- Website: https://leverageedu.com

Jagadis Bose National Science Talent Search (JBNSTS Scholarship)
- Provided by: Jagadis Bose National Science Talent Search, Kolkata
- Eligibility: Students from West Bengal who have completed 12th grade and are pursuing Pure Sciences.
- Application Process: Online application, followed by an aptitude test and interview.
- Deadline: Usually July or August.
- Benefits: Scholarships for undergraduate studies in Basic Sciences.
- Website: https://jbnsts.ac.in

Abroad:

If you're thinking about studying abroad in the US, UK, Australia, Canada, or Germany, here are some excellent scholarship options designed to support students like you pursuing Medical and Health Sciences, Engineering, Pure Sciences, or R&D. These scholarships offer financial aid and opportunities to excel in top universities globally.

United States:

Fulbright Foreign Student Program
- Provided by: The Fulbright Program
- Eligibility: International students with strong academic achievements, leadership potential, and involvement in their community. Ideal for students in Medical Sciences, Engineering, or R&D.
- Application Process: Online application with transcripts and recommendation letters.
- Deadline: Typically, in October (varies by country).
- Benefits: Covers tuition, living expenses, health insurance, and travel costs.
- Website: https://foreign.fulbrightonline.org

AAUW International Fellowships
- Provided by: American Association of University Women (AAUW)
- Eligibility: International women pursuing full-time graduate or postdoctoral studies in Engineering, Health Sciences, Pure Sciences, and related fields.
- Application Process: Submit academic records, recommendation letters, and project proposals.
- Deadline: Typically, in November.
- Benefits: Financial aid ranging from $18,000 to $30,000.
- Website: https://www.aauw.org

United Kingdom:

Rhodes Scholarship
- Provided by: University of Oxford
- Eligibility: Exceptional students with leadership potential and academic excellence, especially in Medical Sciences, Engineering, or R&D.
- Application Process: Submit online applications with essays, recommendation letters, and interviews.
- Deadline: Varies by country.
- Benefits: Full tuition, living expenses, and travel allowances for study at the University of Oxford.
- Website: https://www.rhodeshouse.ox.ac.uk

Chevening Scholarship
- Provided by: The UK Government
- Eligibility: Students with excellent academic records and leadership potential. Open to various fields, including Engineering, Health Sciences, and Pure Sciences.
- Application Process: Online application with academic transcripts, essays, and references.
- Deadline: November.
- Benefits: Full funding for a one-year master's program in the UK, covering tuition, living expenses, and travel.
- Website: https://www.chevening.org

Australia:

Australia Awards Scholarship
- Provided by: The Australian Government
- Eligibility: International students in various fields, including Medical Sciences, Engineering, and Technology. Must demonstrate leadership qualities

and commitment to contributing to their home country.
- Application Process: Apply online, submit academic transcripts, and provide proof of English competence.
- Deadline: Varies by country.
- Benefits: Covers tuition, living expenses, and healthcare.
- Website: https://www.dfat.gov.au

University of Sydney International Scholarships
- Provided by: University of Sydney
- Eligibility: International students pursuing undergraduate or graduate degrees in Medical Sciences, Engineering, or Pure Sciences.
- Application Process: Online application, submission of academic records, and personal statement.
- Deadline: Rolling deadlines, check the official website.
- Benefits: Financial support ranging from partial to full scholarships.
- Website: https://www.sydney.edu.au

Canada:

Vanier Canada Graduate Scholarships
- Provided by: Government of Canada
- Eligibility: Doctoral students in Medical Sciences, Engineering, Pure Sciences, or R&D, with leadership potential and a high standard of academic achievement.
- Application Process: Nominations by Canadian universities, online applications, and references.
- Deadline: November.
- Benefits: $50,000 per year for three years.
- Website: https://vanier.gc.ca

Lester B. Pearson International Scholarships
- Provided by: University of Toronto
- Eligibility: International undergraduate students with outstanding academic achievements and leadership potential. Open to students interested in Science, Engineering, and Medical fields.
- Application Process: Nominated by high schools, with academic records and essays.
- Deadline: January.
- Benefits: Full tuition, books, and residence support for four years.
- Website: https://future.utoronto.ca

Germany:

DAAD Scholarships
- Provided by: German Academic Exchange Service (DAAD)
- Eligibility: International students pursuing Medical Sciences, Engineering, Pure Sciences, or R&D. Strong academic record required
- Application Process: Online application, academic records, research proposal, and recommendation letters.
- Deadline: Varies by program.
- Benefits: Covers tuition, monthly living stipends, and health insurance.
- Website: https://www.daad.de

Heinrich Boll Foundation Scholarships
- Provided by: Heinrich Boll Foundation
- Eligibility: International students in undergraduate, graduate, or doctoral programs in Science, Engineering, Medical fields, or R&D. Focus on academic achievement and social involvement.

- Application Process: Submit academic transcripts, letters of recommendation, and a personal statement.
- Deadline: March and September.
- Benefits: Monthly financial support for living expenses and tuition fees.
- Website: https://www.boell.de

These scholarships not only offer financial assistance but also open doors to world-class educational and research opportunities in some of the best universities globally. Explore each program's requirements, and take a step toward your dream career.

TRAININGS IN INDIA AND ABROAD

If you're looking to explore into your chosen field, enrolling in specialized training programs is a great way to sharpen your skills and gain hands-on experience. Whether you're interested in Medical and Health Sciences, Engineering and Technology, Pure Sciences, or Research & Development (R&D), there's a training program out there for you. Let's explore some exciting opportunities both in India and abroad.

India:

Medical and Health Sciences: AIIMS Summer Research Program
- Topics Covered: Medical research, clinical trials, and public health.
- Duration: 2 months
- Application Process: Apply online through the AIIMS website with your resume and academic records.
- Benefits: Gain valuable experience in healthcare, work with leading doctors, and get exposure to real-world medical challenges.

Engineering: Summer Programs at Indian Institutes of Technology (IITs)
- Topics Covered: AI, robotics, nanotechnology, renewable energy, and more.
- Duration: 4 to 8 weeks
- Application Process: Apply through individual IIT websites with your academic credentials.
- Benefits: Work on innovative projects, learn advanced lab techniques, and connect with top engineers and researchers.

Pure Sciences: National Science Academy Workshops
- Topics Covered: Physics, chemistry, biology, earth sciences.
- Duration: 1 to 7 days
- Application Process: Visit the websites of the National Academy of Sciences India (NASI), Indian Academy of Sciences (IAS), and Indian National Science Academy (INSA) to apply.
- Benefits: Attend lectures by top scientists, get hands-on experience with experiments, and build a strong foundation in the sciences.

Technology: Coding Bootcamps
- Topics Covered: Programming languages (Python, Java), web development, data science, AI, and machine learning.
- Duration: From 1 week to several months.
- Application Process: Apply online through coding schools or platforms like Coding Ninjas or Scaler Academy.
- Benefits: Gain practical skills in coding and programming, and work on real-world projects that can boost your portfolio.

Abroad:

United States:

Medical: Mayo Clinic Summer Research Fellowship
- Topics Covered: Medical research, surgery, and public health.
- Duration: 10 weeks
- Application Process: Apply through the Mayo Clinic website with your resume and a personal statement.
- Benefits: Get exposure to world-class medical research and hands-on experience with clinical practices.

Engineering: MIT Summer Engineering Program
- Topics Covered: Robotics, AI, renewable energy, and space technology.
- Duration: 6 to 8 weeks
- Application Process: Apply through the MIT website with your academic background and project proposal.
- Benefits: Work with leading experts in technology and innovation, and gain experience on real-world engineering challenges.

United Kingdom:

Medical: King's College London Summer School
- Topics Covered: Medicine, clinical research, and healthcare systems.
- Duration: 4 to 6 weeks
- Application Process: Apply through the King's College website with your academic transcripts and personal essay.
- Benefits: Experience top-notch medical training, learn from healthcare experts, and gain a global perspective

on healthcare systems.

Engineering: University of Cambridge Engineering Summer Program
- Topics Covered: Mechanical engineering, renewable energy, and materials science.
- Duration: 4 to 6 weeks
- Application Process: Apply through the university website with your CV and a statement of purpose.
- Benefits: Engage in innovative research, learn advanced engineering techniques, and connect with global experts.

Australia:

Medical: University of Melbourne Health Sciences Internship
- Topics Covered: Public health, epidemiology, and clinical research.
- Duration: 6 to 8 weeks
- Application Process: Apply online through the university's internship portal with your resume and recommendations.
- Benefits: Work with top researchers in health sciences, gain real-world experience, and explore global healthcare solutions.

Technology: University of Sydney Tech Bootcamp
- Topics Covered: Data science, machine learning, and AI.
- Duration: 4 to 8 weeks
- Application Process: Submit your application and transcripts through the university website.
- Benefits: Learn emerging technologies, gain practical coding skills, and work on projects that can make an

impact.

Canada:

Medical: McGill University Health Sciences Research Program

- Topics Covered: Medical research, bioinformatics, and healthcare.
- Duration: 6 to 10 weeks
- Application Process: Apply through the McGill University website with your resume and personal statement.
- Benefits: Engage with innovative research in health sciences, and gain hands-on experience in medical labs.

Engineering: University of Toronto Engineering Internship

- Topics Covered: Civil engineering, software development, renewable energy.
- Duration: 4 to 8 weeks
- Application Process: Apply online with your academic background and project proposal.
- Benefits: Work on innovative engineering projects, connect with professionals, and gain practical experience in your field.

Germany:

Medical: Charite – Universitatsmedizin Berlin Medical Internship

- Topics Covered: Clinical research, surgery, and medical technologies.
- Duration: 6 to 12 weeks
- Application Process: Apply through the university's website with your resume and references.

- Benefits: Learn from one of the leading medical universities in Europe and gain exposure to advanced medical practices.

Engineering: Technical University of Munich Engineering Summer School
- Topics Covered: Robotics, AI, and energy systems.
- Duration: 4 to 8 weeks
- Application Process: Apply online with your academic documents and project ideas.
- Benefits: Work with innovative technology, collaborate with global innovators, and gain hands-on experience in the field.

Quick Reflection!
- Which of these programs aligns with your career goals?
- How can you start preparing for these opportunities today?

These training programs offer an excellent way to build specialized skills and gain real-world experience. Explore the opportunities, start preparing, and take the next step toward crafting your dream career.

RESEARCH GRANTS AND FELLOWSHIPS

Getting funding for research can open doors to amazing opportunities. There are fellowships and grants designed to help students explore scientific projects, even right after completing 10+2. Whether you're interested in Medical and Health Sciences, Engineering, or Pure Sciences, these programs can help you gain valuable experience early on. Let's take a look at some great options in India and abroad.

India:

Indian Academy of Sciences Summer Research Fellowship (IAS, SRFP)
- Who Can Apply: B.Sc. students in fields like Statistics and Mathematics, or second-year students in integrated M.Sc./M.S. programs.
- What You'll Do: Work on exciting summer research projects in top universities across India.
- Why It's Great: You'll get hands-on research experience and a fellowship to support your work.
- Website: https://webjapps.ias.ac.in

Research Internships at IITs
- Who Can Apply: Students who've completed 10+2 or are pursuing their undergraduate degrees.
- What You'll Do: Work on real research projects guided by IIT professors in fields like Engineering, Technology, and Sciences.
- Why It's Great: A chance to contribute to incredible research and gain mentorship from top experts.
- Website: Check individual IIT websites for specific opportunities.

AIIMS Summer Research Programs
- Who Can Apply: Students interested in Medical Sciences.
- What You'll Do: Participate in medical research at AIIMS, one of India's leading medical institutes.
- Why It's Great: Learn from renowned medical professionals and get a deeper understanding of healthcare research.
- Website: Check the AIIMS portal for application details.

IIT Madras Summer Fellowship in Biomedical Engineering
- Who Can Apply: Undergraduates and 10+2 students passionate about Biomedical Engineering.
- What You'll Do: Engage in research that bridges medicine and technology.
- Why It's Great: You'll learn how engineering can advance healthcare through innovation.
- Website: Look for updates on IIT Madras' official site.

Abroad:

United States:

Mayo Clinic Internships for Medical Sciences
- Who Can Apply: Students interested in Medical Research.
- What You'll Do: Work on medical research projects at the world-renowned Mayo Clinic.
- Why It's Great: This is a golden opportunity to be involved in innovative healthcare research.
- Website: https://jobs.mayoclinic.org

Google Research Internship (US)
- Who Can Apply: Students interested in Computer Science or Engineering.
- What You'll Do: Be part of exciting research in AI, machine learning, or other innovative tech fields at Google.
- Why It's Great: You'll work on real-world problems, get mentorship from top engineers, and build skills for your future career.
- Website: https://careers.google.com

United Kingdom:

Wellcome Trust Biomedical Research Internship
- Who Can Apply: Students interested in Medical Sciences and Biomedical Engineering.
- What You'll Do: Conduct research in medical science and work alongside leading healthcare professionals.
- Why It's Great: You'll be part of medical advancements and gain experience in one of the world's best research environments.
- Website: https://wellcome.org

Royal Society Research Fellowships
- Who Can Apply: Students pursuing Engineering, Mathematics, or Pure Sciences.
- What You'll Do: Participate in research projects supported by the Royal Society.
- Why It's Great: This is a renowned fellowship that can boost your academic and research career.
- Website: https://royalsociety.org

Australia:

Australian National University (ANU) Summer Research Program
- Who Can Apply: Students interested in Engineering, Computer Science, or Medical Sciences.
- What You'll Do: Work on research projects in a range of fields from Biomedical Science to Engineering.
- Why It's Great: You'll gain hands-on research experience in one of Australia's top universities.
- Website: https://www.anu.edu.au

University of Sydney Engineering Research Fellowship
- Who Can Apply: Students passionate about Engineering and technology.
- What You'll Do: Participate in innovative projects ranging from robotics to environmental engineering.
- Why It's Great: You'll contribute to innovative technology research while learning from experienced faculty.
- Website: https://www.sydney.edu.au

Canada:

NSERC Undergraduate Student Research Awards (USRA)
- Who Can Apply: Students interested in Engineering, Natural Sciences, or Mathematics.
- What You'll Do: Work on research projects in a range of scientific disciplines at Canadian universities.
- Why It's Great: This award helps you gain valuable research experience while studying in Canada.
- Website: https://www.nserc-crsng.gc.ca

Canadian Institutes of Health Research (CIHR) Internships
- Who Can Apply: Students interested in Medical Sciences or Healthcare Research.
- What You'll Do: Participate in health research that can contribute to public health developments.
- Why It's Great: You'll help improve health outcomes in Canada and beyond.
- Website: https://cihr-irsc.gc.ca

Germany:

Helmholtz Summer Internships
- Who Can Apply: Students in Engineering, Physics, and Medical Sciences.
- What You'll Do: Work with leading researchers on projects ranging from biomedicine to sustainable energy.
- Why It's Great: Germany's research landscape is rich in innovation, and this internship offers a chance to contribute to incredible work.
- Website: https://www.helmholtz.de

Quick Reflection!
- Which of these programs aligns with your goals?
- How can you start preparing today?

Research grants and fellowships are incredible ways to kickstart your career, even if you're just starting out. Whether you're in India or exploring opportunities abroad, these programs can help you grow, gain experience, and make an impact in your chosen field. So, start exploring.

ONLINE LEARNING PLATFORMS

These online platforms are valuable resources to help you build essential skills for various science careers. Whether you're interested in Medical and Health Sciences, Engineering, or Pure Sciences, you'll find flexible, accessible courses to support your career goals. Let's explore them based on where they are available and how they can help in specific fields.

India:

Swayam NPTEL
- Best For: Engineering and Technology
- Description: Created by top Indian institutions like IITs. Swayam NPTEL offers free courses on various topics, including engineering, technology, and medical sciences. These courses are self-paced and perfect for learning the fundamentals of your chosen field. A small fee applies for exams.
- Website: https://onlinecourses.nptel.ac.in

Spoken Tutorial
- Best For: Engineering and Technology, Pure Sciences
- Description: Spoken Tutorial provides video tutorials in subjects like computer programming, data science, and basic engineering concepts, making it a great resource for gaining technical skills. The tutorials are available in various regional languages, making it accessible to many students.
- Website: https://www.spoken-tutorial.org

Khan Academy
- Best For: Medical and Health Sciences, Pure Sciences
- Description: If you need help with high school-level topics like biology, chemistry, or physics, Khan Academy offers free, easy-to-understand courses. It's perfect for building a strong foundation before moving on to specialized fields like medicine or pure sciences.
- Website: https://www.khanacademy.org

Abroad:

United States

Coursera
- Best For: Medical and Health Sciences, Engineering, Pure Sciences
- Description: Coursera partners with top universities around the world to provide courses in medical sciences, engineering, and pure sciences. For medical students, you can find courses on public health, anatomy, and biotechnology, while engineering students can explore AI, computer science, and more. Certifications can help boost your qualifications.
- Website: https://www.coursera.org

MIT Open Courseware
- Best For: Pure Sciences, Engineering
- Description: Access free lecture materials and resources from MIT, one of the world's leading institutions. Pure science students can explore into topics like physics and biology, while engineering students can find materials on mechanical and electrical engineering.
- Website: https://ocw.mit.edu

LinkedIn Learning
- Best For: Engineering, Technology, R&D
- Description: A subscription-based platform, LinkedIn Learning offers courses on data science, software development, and project management. It's a great resource for students aiming to enter fields like software engineering or those interested in research and development.
- Website: https://www.linkedin.com/learning

United Kingdom:

edX
- Best For: Medical and Health Sciences, Engineering
- Description: edX provides courses from top UK universities on subjects like public health, bioinformatics, and environmental science. Engineering students can find courses on topics like robotics and sustainable energy.
- Website: https://www.edx.org

Future Learn
- Best For: Medical and Health Sciences, Pure Sciences
- Description: A flexible learning platform, FutureLearn offers a variety of courses in forensic science, nutrition,

and psychology. It's a great choice for medical science and pure science students looking for in-depth knowledge in specific fields.
- Website: https://www.futurelearn.com

Australia:

Udemy
- Best For: Engineering, Technology
- Description: Udemy is a great platform for short-term, practical courses. It offers numerous programs in programming, data science, and machine learning. Engineering students can also find specialized courses on AI, cloud computing, and software development.
- Website: https://www.udemy.com

DataCamp
- Best For: R&D, Engineering
- Description: For students interested in data science or R&D, DataCamp is the go-to platform. It offers hands-on courses in data analysis, statistics, and machine learning with practical exercises.
- Website: https://www.datacamp.com

Canada:

Coursera
- Best For: Medical and Health Sciences, Pure Sciences
- Description: Coursera is also highly popular in Canada, offering courses from Canadian universities on topics like healthcare systems, biomedical engineering, and ecology. It's perfect for students aiming to build a career in medical or pure sciences.
- Website: https://www.coursera.org

LinkedIn Learning
- Best For: Technology, R&D
- Description: Similar to the US, LinkedIn Learning provides Canadian students with courses on coding, data science, and project management. It's ideal for those entering technology or working in R&D.
- Website: https://www.linkedin.com/learning

Germany:

MIT Open Courseware
- Best For: Pure Sciences, Engineering
- Description: Widely used by students in Germany as well, MIT Open Courseware is a fantastic resource for those interested in physics, chemistry, or mechanical engineering. It's completely free and available globally.
- Website: https://ocw.mit.edu

edX
- Best For: Medical and Health Sciences, Engineering
- Description: edX offers courses from top universities around the world, including Germany, on medical research, engineering, and environmental science. It's ideal for students aiming to pursue a career in either medical or engineering fields.
- Website: https://www.edx.org

Quick Reflection!
Which course do you think would benefit you the most in your career journey?

How These Platforms Support Your Career Path

- Medical and Health Sciences: Platforms like Coursera, edX, and FutureLearn offer specialized courses in medical research, public health, and bioinformatics. These courses will help you build a strong foundation in medical sciences and health technology.

- Engineering and Technology: For aspiring engineers, platforms like Swayam NPTEL, MIT Open Courseware, and Udemy provide industry-relevant courses on robotics, AI, and programming.

- Pure Sciences: Students interested in biology, physics, and chemistry will find valuable resources on Khan Academy, MIT Open Courseware, and edX to strengthen their knowledge and explore advanced topics.

- R&D: DataCamp and LinkedIn Learning are perfect for students keen on research and development. These platforms offer specialized courses in data science, statistics, and machine learning, which are essential for innovative research work.

By utilizing these platforms, you can gain the skills and knowledge needed to succeed in your chosen field, whether it's medicine, engineering, or pure sciences. Each of these platforms offers something unique to help you craft your dream career.

PROFESSIONAL ASSOCIATIONS AND SOCIETIES

Becoming a member of professional associations is a fantastic way to grow your network and stay ahead in your field. These groups help you make valuable connections, gain access to exclusive resources, and attend events that can boost your career. You'll stay updated on the latest trends and developments, meet like-minded professionals, and open doors to new opportunities.

To make it easier, we've categorized these associations based on different fields and included both India-based and International associations, highlighting how they can help you in your career path.

India:

Medical and Health Sciences:

Indian Association of Physiotherapists (IAP)
- Website: https://www.physiotherapyindia.org
- Great for those pursuing a career in physiotherapy,

offering access to research, certifications, and networking opportunities within the medical field.

Indian Society for Cell Biology (ISCB)
- Website: https://iscb.co.in
- Perfect for students interested in biological research. It provides updates on the latest developments in cell biology and opportunities to collaborate on projects.

Indian Society of Genetics and Plant Breeding (ISGPB)
- Website: https://www.isgpb.org
- Ideal for those focusing on genetic research or plant science, offering conferences and publications on innovative research.

Engineering and Technology:

Indian Society for Technical Education (ISTE)
- Website: https://www.isteonline.in
- This society is essential for engineering students. You'll gain access to workshops, training programs, and research papers, helping you stay ahead in the tech world.

Indian Society of Structural Engineers (ISSE)
- Website: https://isse.org.in
- For aspiring civil and structural engineers, this organization offers insights into the latest engineering techniques and industry standards.

Computer Society of India (CSI)
- Website: https://www.csiindia.org
- If you're passionate about computer science and IT, CSI provides resources for professional development and keeps you updated on technological trends.

Pure Sciences:

Indian Science Congress Association (ISCA)
- Website: https://www.sciencecongress.nic.in
- An excellent association for all science enthusiasts. It offers the chance to present research papers and interact with leading scientists across various disciplines.

Indian National Science Academy (INSA)
- Website: https://www.insaindia.res.in
- Perfect for students passionate about research in the natural sciences. You'll have access to publications and conferences on new discoveries.

Indian Academy of Sciences (IAS)
- Website: https://www.ias.ac.in
- Focused on promoting scientific knowledge, this academy offers fellowships, summer programs, and conferences in all fields of pure science.

Abroad:

United States:

American Medical Association (AMA)
- Website: https://www.ama-assn.org
- For those pursuing medical careers, AMA provides guidance on certifications, internships, and research opportunities.

Institute of Electrical and Electronics Engineers (IEEE)
- Website: https://www.ieee.org
- Ideal for students interested in electrical engineering and electronics. IEEE offers access to technical

papers, industry trends, and global networking events.

United Kingdom:

Institute of Biomedical Science (IBMS)
- Website: https://www.ibms.org
- For biomedical science students, IBMS provides training, conferences, and certification opportunities to enhance your career.

Royal Society of Chemistry (RSC)
- Website: https://www.rsc.org
- If chemistry is your field of interest, RSC offers access to journals, conferences, and research grants to deepen your knowledge.

Australia:

Engineers Australia
- Website: https://www.engineersaustralia.org.au
- Essential for engineering students, this association offers accreditation, internships, and networking opportunities across Australia.

Australian Medical Association (AMA)
- Website: https://ama.com.au
- A great resource for those in medical careers, providing news on medical developments, policies, and research opportunities.

Canada:

Canadian Society for Medical Laboratory Science (CSMLS)
- Website: https://www.csmls.org
- For students interested in medical laboratory science, this society provides certifications and up-to-date knowledge on lab practices.

Canadian Mathematical Society (CMS)
- Website: https://www.cms.math.ca
- If you love mathematics, CMS offers conferences, publications, and collaborative research opportunities.

Germany:

German Medical Association (Bundesarztekammer)
- Website: https://www.bundesaerztekammer.de
- For students entering the medical field, this association offers important resources on health policies, research, and certifications in Germany.

German Association of Engineers (VDI)
- Website: https://www.vdi.de
- For those interested in engineering, VDI provides access to the latest innovations, industry insights, and networking opportunities.

Quick Reflection!
- How can joining these associations enhance your knowledge and connect you with experts to guide your career path?
- What's your next step in becoming an active member?

GOVERNMENT INITIATIVES AND PROGRAMS

Let's explore some fantastic government programs designed to support students passionate about science and research. These initiatives are perfect for high school graduates who want to explore careers in Medical and Health Sciences, Engineering and Technology, Pure Sciences, or Research and Development (R&D). These programs encourage critical thinking and offer financial aid, research opportunities, and mentorship to students who want to explore the exciting world of science.

India:

INSPIRE (Innovation in Science Pursuit for Inspired Research)
- Field: Pure Sciences
- Offered by: Department of Science and Technology (DST), India
- Benefits: INSPIRE is a great opportunity for students

interested in Pure Sciences. It offers scholarships, mentorship, and exposure to research in top institutions across India.
- Eligibility: For high school students aiming for bachelor's or master's degrees in basic sciences.
- Website: https://www.inspire.dst.gov.in

Abroad:

United States

Research Experiences for Undergraduates (REU)
- Field: Engineering, Technology, R&D
- Offered by: National Science Foundation (NSF)
- Benefits: REU provides hands-on research experience for students interested in Engineering, Technology, or R&D fields. Students work under expert guidance on advanced research projects.
- Eligibility: Undergraduate students in STEM fields.
- Website: https://www.nsf.gov/crssprgm/reu

Canada:

Undergraduate Student Research Awards (USRA)
- Field: Engineering, Pure Sciences
- Offered by: Natural Sciences and Engineering Research Council (NSERC)
- Benefits: USRA is ideal for students in Engineering and Pure Sciences. It offers hands-on research experience, funding, and the chance to collaborate with top researchers.
- Eligibility: Undergraduate students pursuing studies in science or engineering.
- Website:https://www.nserc-crsng.gc.ca/Students-Etudiants/UG-PC/USRA-BRPC_eng.asp

Australia:

Indigenous STEM Awards
- Field: STEM (Science, Technology, Engineering, Math)
- Offered by: Commonwealth Scientific and Industrial Research Organisation (CSIRO)
- Benefits: This program is fantastic for students passionate about STEM fields, offering financial support, mentorship, and opportunities to participate in STEM-related activities.
- Eligibility: High school graduates interested in STEM fields.
- Website:https://www.csiro.au/en/about/facilities-and-collections/indigenous-stem-awards

Germany:

German Academic Exchange Service (DAAD) Scholarships
- Field: Medical, Engineering, Pure Sciences
- Offered by: DAAD (Deutscher Akademischer Austauschdienst)
- Benefits: DAAD offers scholarships to students in Medical, Engineering, and Pure Sciences who want to study or conduct research in Germany. It's a great chance to explore international opportunities in innovative fields.
- Eligibility: Open to international students, especially for those pursuing master's or PhD programs.
- Website: https://www.daad.de/en/

United Kingdom:

Newton International Fellowships
- Field: Medical, Engineering, Pure Sciences, R&D
- Offered by: The Royal Society
- Benefits: Newton Fellowships provide an excellent platform for postdoctoral students in Medical, Engineering, Pure Sciences, and R&D to engage in research collaborations in the UK.
- Eligibility: Open to early career researchers from around the world.
- Website: https://royalsociety.org/grants-schemes-awards/grants/newton-international/

Quick Reflection!
How can joining one of these programs or initiatives help you gain practical experience, connect with professionals in your field, and enhance your career opportunities?

These programs help promote the next generation of scientists and researchers by offering valuable opportunities to explore and contribute to the exciting world of scientific discovery.

EXPLORING TOP UNIVERSITIES FOR YOUR DREAM CAREER

As you begin your journey to craft your dream career, choosing the right university can be an essential step. This guide highlights some of the top universities in India and abroad, organized by the fields relevant to your interests- Medical and Health Sciences, Engineering and Technology, Pure Sciences, and R&D. Each university offers unique programs and opportunities that can help you gain the knowledge and skills needed to succeed in your chosen path.

India:

Indian Institute of Technology (IIT)
- Known for: Engineering and Technology, R&D
- Website: https://www.iitsystem.ac.in/

All India Institute of Medical Sciences (AIIMS)
- Known for: Medical and Health Sciences
- Website: https://www.aiims.edu/

Indian Institute of Science (IISc)
- Known for: R&D, Pure Sciences, Engineering
- Website: https://www.iisc.ac.in/

Jawaharlal Nehru University (JNU)
- Known for: Medical Sciences, Pure Sciences
- Website: https://www.jnu.ac.in/

Post Graduate Institute of Medical Education and Research (PGIMER)
- Known for: Medical and Health Sciences
- Website: https://pgimer.edu.in/

United States:

Harvard University
- Known for: Medical and Health Sciences, Pure Sciences
- Website: https://www.harvard.edu/

Stanford University
- Known for: Engineering and Technology, R&D
- Website: https://www.stanford.edu/

Massachusetts Institute of Technology (MIT)
- Known for: Engineering, Technology, Pure Sciences, R&D
- Website: https://www.mit.edu/

California Institute of Technology (Caltech)
- Known for: Pure Sciences, Engineering
- Website: https://www.caltech.edu/

University of Chicago
- Known for: Social Sciences, Biological Sciences
- Website: https://www.uchicago.edu/

United Kingdom:

University of Oxford
- Known for: Medical and Health Sciences, Pure Sciences
- Website: https://www.ox.ac.uk/

Imperial College London
- Known for: Engineering and Technology, R&D
- Website: https://www.imperial.ac.uk/

University of Cambridge
- Known for: Medical Sciences, Engineering
- Website: https://www.cam.ac.uk/

London School of Economics and Political Science (LSE)
- Known for: Social Sciences, R&D
- Website: https://www.lse.ac.uk/

University College London (UCL)
- Known for: Medical and Health Sciences, Engineering
- Website: https://www.ucl.ac.uk/

Australia:

University of Melbourne
- Known for: Medical and Health Sciences, Engineering, R&D
- Website: https://www.unimelb.edu.au/

Australian National University (ANU)
- Known for: Pure Sciences, Engineering
- Website: https://www.anu.edu.au/

University of Sydney
- Known for: Medical and Health Sciences, Engineering
- Website: https://www.sydney.edu.au/

University of Queensland (UQ)
- Known for: Medical and Health Sciences, R&D
- Website: https://www.uq.edu.au/

Monash University
- Known for: Medical and Health Sciences, Engineering
- Website: https://www.monash.edu/

Canada:

University of Toronto
- Known for: Medical Sciences, Pure Sciences
- Website: https://www.utoronto.ca/

University of British Columbia (UBC)
- Known for: Engineering, R&D
- Website: https://www.ubc.ca/

McGill University
- Known for: Medical and Health Sciences, Pure Sciences
- Website: https://www.mcgill.ca/

University of Alberta
- Known for: Engineering, R&D
- Website: https://www.ualberta.ca/

McMaster University
- Known for: Medical and Health Sciences, R&D
- Website: https://www.mcmaster.ca/

Germany:

Technical University of Munich (TUM)
- Known for: Engineering, Technology, R&D
- Website: https://www.tum.de/

Heidelberg University
- Known for: Medical and Health Sciences, Pure Sciences
- Website: https://www.uni-heidelberg.de/

RWTH Aachen University
- Known for: Engineering, R&D
- Website: https://www.rwth-aachen.de/

University of Freiburg
- Known for: Medical Sciences, R&D
- Website: https://www.uni-freiburg.de/

Karlsruhe Institute of Technology (KIT)
- Known for: Engineering, Pure Sciences
- Website: https://www.kit.edu/

Quick Reflection!
- Which field are you most passionate about?
- How could these university programs help you achieve your dream career?

These universities offer a wealth of programs tailored to your career goals. By exploring the options available in each field, you can find the right path to help you achieve your dream career. Remember, education is a powerful tool in shaping your future.

REFERENCES

https://www.ncs.gov.in

https://www.coursera.org

https://www.ncda.org

https://www.bio.org

https://www.themuse.com/advice/how-to-change-careers

https://www.ted.com/speakers/gordon_ramsay

https://www.bbc.com/news/world-asia-india-23093313

https://people.com/celebrity/zendaya-and-her-close-knit-family/

https://www.bbc.com/news/world-asia-india-27646048

https://www.nature.com/subjects/bioinformatics

https://www.britannica.com/biography/APJ-Abdul-Kalam

https://www.paulocoelhoblog.com/

https://www.linkedin.com/learning/

https://www.edx.org/

https://www.espn.com

https://www.forbes.com

https://elearningindustry.com/technology-role-continuous-learning-development

https://www.simplilearn.com/top-tech-skills-for-future-article

https://www.mindsetworks.com/science/

https://www.ncbi.nlm.nih.gov/pmc/articles/PMC6491928/

WE NEED YOUR FEEDBACK

Dear Readers,

Your feedback truly matters to me as I aim to support students in finding their way after 10+2. It's more than just a review-your words can inspire and guide countless young people. Please take a moment to share your thoughts. Together, we can help families make informed, life-changing decisions for their futures.

If you're interested in more insights, check out my next book, **"Crafting Your Dream Career: A 3 Step Roadmap to Building a Rewarding Interdisciplinary Science Career after 10+2"**. This book systematically explores exciting **interdisciplinary** career paths, gaining insights into qualifications, growth opportunities, academic Programmes, job opportunities, top companies, salaries, renowned universities, and essential skills for each field. Real-life success stories for your exploration.

Click here for more details:

https://www.amazon.in/gp/product/B0CZH5135G

Your feedback on my earlier work means so much to me. Please share your thoughts and help shape the future of my content. Thank you for being a part of this journey of exploration and growth!

What next.......

This book has given you the first steps toward your dream career. We've explored four exciting paths, from medical science and healthcare to research and development.

In the next book, get ready to dive into even more career options! We'll explore fields like data science, artificial intelligence, material science, and so much more. There's a world of possibilities waiting for you—let's keep the journey going!

ABOUT THE AUTHOR

Dr. Swarnangini Sinha is an enthusiastic educator and career mentor, currently serving as Professor in the University. With a Ph.D. in Computer Science and Engineering, she specializes in areas such as Data Mining and Machine Learning.

Dr. Sinha understands the mix of excitement and confusion that comes after completing 10+2. Drawing from her own experiences, she is deeply committed to helping students explore their career options. This series, titled **"Career Planning and Guidance,"** shines a light on the countless opportunities available in science careers. Covering seven main areas—from well-known fields like marine biology to emerging fields like artificial intelligence and sustainable development—these 12 books will help you find where your interests can lead you.

As Dr. Sinha says, **"Every student has the power to create their future; they just need the right guidance to see what's possible."**

The first book, **"Crafting Your Dream Career,"** is your trusted guide on this journey. It's packed with helpful advice and simple steps to help you make informed choices about your future. Whether you're starting to think about your career or looking for a new direction, this book is here to support you.

Let's explore the amazing paths waiting for you!

www.ingramcontent.com/pod-product-compliance
Lightning Source LLC
Chambersburg PA
CBHW071525220526
45469CB00003B/656